Designing & Aligning Employee Benefits Globally

By Cedric Ng Mong Shen

Copyright Cedric Ng Mong Shen 2020

Praise for
"Designing & Aligning Employee Benefits Globally" book

This is a practical approach to reviewing your benefits packages in a balanced manner between where you want to be in the market, what your employees' value, and the cost impact (savings or redistribution between elements or new budget requirement).
By Sandrine Bardot
Award-winning Total Reward expert at The Bardot Group
United Arab Emirates

This book gave me some good ideas on how to consider benefits changes by engaging with employees. I recommend reading it.
By Simone De Luca (GRP, CIPD)
Total Rewards Manager (EMEA and APAC) at Verifone
Italy

This is a very well written and articulated book! Benefits can be a complex arena; however, the author does a nice job laying things out so that even a novice can understand. The book contains labor laws to consider, industry practices, cost considerations and perceived value.
By Stephanie Baker
Total Rewards at Franciscan Health
United States

While salary plays a part in employee engagement, other financial/non-financial benefit play a major role too. Organizations have the buying power to get large discounts in various benefits like car lease, health insurance, etc. But then, how many organizations provide what employees need? Different country and employee population will have different wants and needs to a benefit; how can organizations find out what benefit to provide; how much should the organization spend in benefit to get an ROI in employee engagement or having it incorporated into their EVP? This book provides you the know-how to design an effective benefit plan.
By Nicholas Chew
Consultant, Reward & People Analytics at MLC Life Insurance
Australia

Table of Contents

Table of Contents 3
1) Introduction 5
2) Why give employee benefits? 8
   2.1) Hygiene factors 8
   2.2) Motivation factors 8
3) Measuring the Business impact of employee benefits 11
4) Global Benefits Philosophies 15
5) Global Benefits Strategies for different scenarios 17
6) Employer Branding with Signature Benefits 19
7) Flexi-benefits 21
8) Factors influencing Benefits Globally 22
   8.1) Labor Laws 23
   8.2) Industry practice 23
   8.3) Perceived value 23
   8.4) Costs 23
   8.5) Demographic changes 23
   8.6) Trade Blocs 24
   8.7) Tax laws impacting benefits - Globally 25
      (i) Transport benefits tax – by Country 25
      (ii) Meal benefits tax – by Country 34
      (iii) Housing benefits tax – by Country 35
9) Categories of Benefits 42
   9.1) Income Protection Plans 43
      9.1.1) Healthcare benefits 43
      Medical plans 48
      Dental plans 48
      Vision plans 48
      Hearing plans 48
      9.1.2) Welfare benefits 49
      Death benefits 49
      Disability benefits 49
      9.1.3) Retirement and Investment Plans 50
      9.1.4) Defined benefit (DB) plans 50
      9.1.5) Defined contribution (DC) plans worldwide 51

- 9.2) Pay for time not worked 53
  - Annual leave legislation worldwide 55
  - Sick leave legislation worldwide 56
  - Maternity leave legislation worldwide 57
- 10) How to read employees benefits survey reports 58
  - Survey Report Example 1: Leave Benefits 58
  - Survey Report Example 2: Car Benefits 59
  - Survey Report Example 3: Life and Disability Insurance 60
  - Survey Report Example 4: Clinical Care Coverage 60
- 11) Employees benefits reports - Globally 61
  - (i) Housing allowance - by Country 61
  - (ii) Housing rental prices - by Country 63
  - (iii) Car mileage claim rate – by Country 67
  - (iv) Motorcycle mileage claim rate – by Country 70
  - (v) Petrol prices – by Country 73
  - (vi) Correlation between Petrol prices & Car mileage claim rate - Correlation 75
  - (vii) Relationship between Car & Motorcycle mileage claim rate 76
  - (viii) Winter Clothing benefits – by Country 77
  - (viii) Winter period & temperature – by country 79
- 12) How to review employee benefits – Method 1 82
  - 12.1) Benefits Review Example 1: Brunei employee benefits proposal 82
  - 12.2 Benefits Review Example 2: Singapore employee benefits proposal 83
- 13) How to review employee benefits – Method 2 (MPEP model) 84
  - 13.1) "Market Position" (MP) 86
  - 13.2) "Employee Preference" (EP) 89
  - 13.3) "Benefits Costing" 90
  - 13.4) "Arrows" 90
- 14) Conclusion. 91
- Publications by the Author 92
- Index 99

1) Introduction

Your CEO returned from a management retreat with a new strategic business plan that will revitalize the company and lead it into lucrative new markets. As the Global Rewards Director, you are tasked with designing & aligning employee benefits globally, across different business units and countries. --- Do you know what to do?

Employee Benefits reflect the culture of the organization and differentiate its Employer brand. A company without differentiated Benefits Strategy is like a ship that follows where the wind blows without any direction of its own. This book teaches you how to formulate global employee benefits philosophy and strategies, how to review benefits, how to minimize employee benefits taxes worldwide, and what are the employee benefits requirements worldwide.

1) Develop a Global Employee Benefits Philosophy. Learn how to develop a Global Benefits Philosophy that is broad enough to apply across different business units and countries, and at the same time allow the countries flexibility for customization to local laws, practices and needs.

2) Develop Employee Benefits Strategies for different scenarios. Learn how to develop Employee Benefits Strategies based on your company branding (unbranded, branded), employee performance, job grades, business strategy (Innovation, Value-for-money, Service), business stage (startup, growth, mature, decline)

3) Introduce Signature Benefits for Employer Branding. Develop signature employee benefits that are unique, meaningful, and set your company apart from their competitors.

4) How to minimize employee benefits tax worldwide. Learn what are the tax laws affecting employee benefits for various countries, and how to minimize tax.

5) Learn what are the Employee benefits statutory requirement worldwide. Learn what are the statutory requirement for the provision of employee benefits such as annual leave, sick leave, maternity leave.

6) Benefits market practices worldwide. Learn what are the benefits practices in various countries. E.g. housing allowance, car & motorcycle mileage claim rate, winter clothing benefits, etc.

7) How to read employee survey reports. Learn how to read employee survey report. E.g. Leave benefits, car benefits, life and disability insurance, clinical care coverage.

8) How to review employee benefits for various countries. Do you have difficulty getting Union buy-in to reduce employee benefits? Do you have difficulty convincing your CEO to enhance employee benefits? Do you have difficulty explaining why company can't give employees cash allowances instead of benefits? Learn how to recommend employee benefits changes considering Market-Position, Employee-Preference, & Benefits Cost, to address these issues. Learn how to review employee benefits for various countries (e.g. Brunei, Singapore)

Employee benefits represent a considerable portion of the total rewards package and thus a significant expense to the organization. The importance of the benefits function is highlighted in its role of attracting and retaining employees and fulfilling employee needs. Regardless of the country, benefits serve the same essential functions. Benefits supplement remuneration by providing employees with a level of security related specifically to health and welfare, retirement and time off.

While employee needs may be similar around the world, the degree to which those needs are met through other courses varies by country. Governmental programs and country culture contribute to a variance in the demand for certain benefits. Many differences in benefits practices relate to the extent of governments involvement in providing retirement and medical security to its citizens. In some countries, the influence of government is pronounced (e.g. Chile, Malaysia). Thus, the level of benefits provided by employers often is directly related to the level provided by or mandated by the government. Additionally, the influence of government, labour and other factors tends to either augment or hinder the process of providing employee benefits. This chapter will address many of these influences and cover some of the current trends in global benefits.

Benefits are a core part of the total rewards model. Benefits includes health and welfare plans, retirement plans and programs providing pay for time not worked. Overtime, employee benefits have evolved from basic "fringe benefits" of insurance coverage and a few perquisites to a wide range of benefits to strike a balance between an employee's personal and professional life.

2) Why give employee benefits?

Money can make employees unhappy if they are not sufficiently compensated, but it has not been shown to lead to motivation, satisfaction or performance. Organizations that offers better than average benefits may pay less salary and still have motivated, contributing employees.

There are a host of competing ideas among theorists about what motivates employees. Mainstream theories of employee motivation emphasize intrinsic rewards as being central to the motivation process, while extrinsic rewards are often seen as necessary but not sufficient.

Frederick Herzberg's two-factor theory (also known as Herzberg's motivation-hygiene theory) states that there are certain factors in the workplace that cause job satisfaction, while a separate set of factors cause dissatisfaction. Frederick Herzberg's Two-factor theory distinguishes between: Hygiene factors & Motivation factors.

2.1) Hygiene factors
Hygiene factors are needed to ensure that an employee does not become dissatisfied. Examples of Hygiene factors are employee benefits, salary, work environment, and relationship with peers.

2.2) Motivation factors
Motivation factors are needed to motivate an employee into higher performance. Examples of Motivation factors are interesting job, recognition, and career growth.

The Herzberg's two-factor theory can be linked to employee benefits market positioning as shown in the diagram. Cost conscious companies often say they can't afford to offer benefits, but the reality is, company cannot afford not to. Employee benefits are considered Hygiene factors, and most countries have laws stipulating the minimum benefits that companies must provide. If companies provide employee benefits below what the market is giving, employees will be dissatisfied and unmotivated. Annual leave, Sick leave, and maternity leave aren't just luxuries that would make our lives more pleasant--they're essential. Employees need leave to take care of their own health needs, and moms needs paid time off to care for sick kids. Other consequences of employee dissatisfaction include absenteeism and high employee turnover, both very costly for businesses. If companies provide employee benefits at the same level as what the market is giving, employees will not be dissatisfied, but they will still be unmotivated. Employee benefits become motivation factors if companies provide above-market employee benefits that employees value most. Although some theorists argue that material factors have only a superficial impact on motivation, for certain individuals in certain scenarios, certain company benefits can lead to great motivation.

Figure 1: Relationship between "Herzberg two-factor theory" & "Employee benefits positioning"

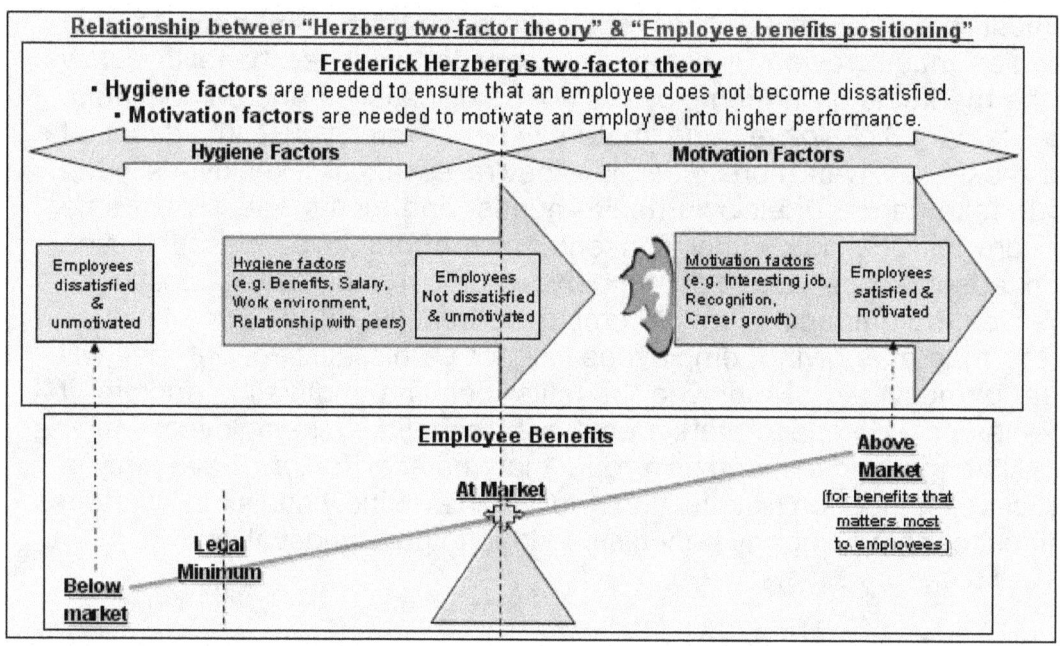

3) Measuring the Business impact of employee benefits

Research have shown that Employee Benefits can impact your organization's absenteeism, performance, job satisfaction, and retention.

Impact on Absenteeism
- In 2005, Royal adopted an incentive scheme where workers with a clean attendance sheet were eligible for prize draws with cars, holidays and gift vouchers. Its sickness absence rates fell by 1%, after the cash incentives was introduced. [1]

Impact on Performance
- A global technology company discovered that there is a direct correlation between the turnover of high performer and compensation. The issue was not just paying employees more, but paying them differently. The statisticians discovered that midlevel performers, who loved working at the company, would not resign even if their salary increases were as low as 90 percent of industry average. However high performers (i.e. top ten percent of employees) were much more sensitive, and will very likely resign when their annual raises were not at least 115 percent of the industry average. [2]
- A study by Harvard and Syracuse Universities on green-certified buildings found employees had 30% fewer headaches and respiratory complaints in the green office environment. The study also showed employees performed nearly 27% better on cognitive tasks. Finally, workers in the study slept better at night, tracked by a wristband measuring sleep quality. [3]

Impact on Job Satisfaction

Chidiebere Ogbonnaya, Kevin Daniels, and Karina Nielsen published a study on how incentive pay (Performance-related pay, Profit-related pay, and Share ownership) affects employees' experience of well-being, as measured by job satisfaction, organizational commitment, and trust in management. [4]

- **Performance-related pay** – The study showed that performance-related pay was positively associated with job satisfaction, organizational commitment, and trust in management.
- **Profit-related pay** - Positive effects of Profit-related pay depends on the extent that profit-related pay is given to a large proportion of the workforce. When employee participation in profit-related pay is high, and where organizational profits are perceived to be equitably distributed, more employees benefit and thus experience job satisfaction, organizational commitment, and trust in management. When the extend of employee participation in Profit-related pay is low to medium, the study found lower levels of job satisfaction, organizational commitment, and trust in management.
- **Share ownership** - the study found that share ownership has a negative relationship with job satisfaction and no relationships with employees' commitment and trust in management. High employee uptake of share ownership also revealed no relationships with employee well-being.

Impact on Retention

- In 2011, two Hewlett-Packard (HP) scientists analyzed two years data and generated Flight Risk score. Flight Risk score predicts the probability of leaving of each of HP's 300,000 employees. Higher pay, promotions and better performance ratings, where negatively related to flight risk. However, there is a complicated relationship between these findings. For example, when an employee got a promotion but did not get a substantial pay raise, this employee would still be more likely to quit. [5]
- Google has always been on the forefront of predictive analytics. Through researched data and historical patterns Google found that new salespeople, who do not get a promotion within four years, are much more likely to leave the company. [6]
- A survey by TechnologyAdvice found that 56 percent of employees said perks were very or moderately important when evaluating a job, and 56 percent of employees say they would trade a salary increase for certain on-the-job perks. [7]
- According to a study by Culture Amp on retention intention at Box, a worker's pay or relationship with his boss matters far less than how connected the worker feels to his team. [8]
- 80 percent of Americans would choose a job with benefits over an identical job that offered 30 percent more salary but no benefits. [9]
- According to the 2018 Aflac study, more than half (55%) of employees surveyed would be at least somewhat likely to accept a job with lower compensation but a more robust benefits package. [10]
- 45% of employees said they consider a prospective company's work-life balance a crucial factor when researching a job. [11]
- 78% of employees said they are more likely to stay with their employer because of their benefit program. [12]
- 42% of businesses report that their ability to recruit and retain employees has been improved by their pension scheme. [13]

References:
(1) Alison Coleman (2011) How incentives help reduce sickness absence. https://www.employeebenefits.co.uk/issues/june-2011/how-incentives-help-reduce-sickness-absence/ (20 November 2018)

(2) Josh Bersin (2014) Deloitte Review issue 14: The datafication of HR https://www2.deloitte.com/insights/us/en/deloitte-review/issue-14/dr14-datafication-of-hr.html (11 November 2018)

(3) Libby Sander (2017) Research shows if you improve the air quality at work, you improve productivity. (26 November 2018)

(4) Chidiebere Ogbonnaya, Kevin Daniels, Karina Nielsen (2017) How Incentive Pay Affects Employee Engagement, Satisfaction, and Trust. Harvard Business Review. https://hbr.org/2017/03/research-how-incentive-pay-affects-employee-engagement-satisfaction-and-trust (18 Oct 2018)

(5) Erik van Vulpen, Predictive Analytics in Human Resources - Tutorial and 7 case studies, https://www.analyticsinhr.com/blog/predictive-analytics-human-resources/
(24 September 2018)

(6) Tom McKeown, Snapshots in Time (2017), https://www.trendata.com/snapshots-in-time/
(24 September 2018)

(7) Savita V Jayaram (2016), The Correlation between Benefits and Employee Retention http://www.hrinasia.com/employee-retention/the-correlation-between-benefits-and-employee-retention/ (27 September 2018)

(8) Rachel Emma Silverman and Nikki Waller (2015) The Algorithm That Tells the Boss Who Might Quit. https://www.visier.com/the-algorithm-that-tells-the-boss-who-might-quit/ (26 November 2018)

(9) AICPA (2018) Americans Favor Workplace Benefits 4 to 1 over Extra Salary: AICPA Survey. https://www.hrmetricsservice.org/wp-content/uploads/2013/07/HR-Metrics-Service-Standards-and-Glossary-v9.6.pdf (19 June 2019)

(10) HR Daily Advisor (2018) Research Shows Strong Job Satisfaction, Benefits https://hrdailyadvisor.blr.com/2018/10/12/research-shows-strong-job-satisfaction-benefits/?source=HAC&effort=44&utm_source=BLR&utm_medium=Email&utm_campaign=HRDAEmail&emailid=4332938&spMailingID=14465349&spUserID=MjU3NzE4NTEzNzYwS0&spJobID=1501512298&spReportId=MTUwMTUxMjI5OAS2 (19 June 2019)

(11) Access Perks (2018) 2018 Employee Benefits and Perks Statistics https://blog.accessperks.com/2018-employee-benefits-perks-statistics (19 June 2019)

(12) Willis Towers Watson (2018) Employees are more likely to stay with their employers when offered a group benefit marketplace https://www.willistowerswatson.com/en-US/insights/2018/08/employee-and-employer-satisfaction-with-group-benefit-marketplaces-survey-results (19 June 2019)

(13) CBI (2018) Workplace pensions engagement isn't a 'nice-to-have', but a fundamental to helping employees plan for later life https://www.cbi.org.uk/media-centre/articles/workplace-pensions-engagement-isnt-a-nice-to-have-but-a-fundamental-to-helping-employees-plan-for-later-life/ (19 June 2019)

4) Global Benefits Philosophies

The Global Benefits Philosophy should provide guidance on decision making, and be broad enough to apply across different business units and countries. **It should specify the competitive position of its benefits (E.g. 75th percentile for employee wellness, 50th percentile for other benefits).** A company's budget also plays a large part in determining which benefits it can offer globally.

Employee Benefits such as share plans, product discounts, fitness benefits, recognition schemes, can be implemented worldwide, but others, such as retrenchment benefits and annual leave, will differ between countries based on local labor laws. Examples of Global Benefits Philosophies that can be applied across different business units and countries are:

- **Foster employee wellness.**
    - Employee wellness related benefits at 75th percentile of market
    - Hydraulic Tables for office employees
    - Dependent benefits
    - Free family counselling hotline
    - Health/Stress Talks
    - Under-Desk cycling exercise machine
    - Life insurance cover of at least 1 x annual salary

- **Financial security for our employees**.
    - Employee financial security related benefits at 75th percentile of market
    - Provide every employee worldwide with at least three-times salary life cover, because we believe that it is important, and because we care about the dependents of our employees.

- **Work-life balance**.
    - Work-life balance related benefits at 75th percentile of market
    - Work from home options for office workers.

- **Fun workplace**.
    - Help employees make friends at work through Free snacks at pantry, Buddy system, Team building events, staff birthday celebrations, provision of communication tools like skype.

- **Foster appreciation and recognition.**
    - Make recognition part of the culture worldwide,
    - Provide recognitions options (Thank you email templates),
    - Share recognition ideas (E.g. drive by to visit your colleagues to catch up with their lives, handwritten recognition notes, grab a team member for a quick walk and talk over coffee).

5) Global Benefits Strategies for different scenarios

Rewards Strategy and Company Branding

	Unbranded startup	Branded startup	Established company
Salary	High	Mid to high	Mid to high
Benefits	Low	Low	Mid
Short term incentives	Low to high	High	High
Long term incentives	Nil to high	High	Mid

Rewards Strategy and Employee's potential

	Low performer	Average performer	High potential
Salary	P25	P50	P75
Pay increase speed	Slow	Average	Fast
Short term incentives	Low	Average	High
Long term incentives	Nil	Average	High
Benefits	Average	Average	High
Training	Low	Average	High
Career progression	Low	Average	High

Rewards Strategy and Job Grade

	Top Management	Senior Management	Middle Management	Professionals	Rank and file
Salary	Mid	Mid	High	High	Low
Benefits	High	Mid to high	Mid	Mid	Low
Short term incentives	High	High	Mid	Mid	Low
Long term incentives	High	High	Nil to low	Nil	Nill

Rewards Strategy and Business Strategy

	Product leadership	Value for money	Customer Service
Salary	P75	P25	P50
Benefits	P75	P25	P75
Incentives	Reward Innovation	P50	Reward Customer Service Excellence
Job descriptions	Flexible job descriptions	Clearly defined job descriptions and processes	More decision making autonomy to enable employees to solve problems faster
Employee traits	• Agile • Risk taking • Innovative	• Cost consciousness	• Conscientiousness • Extraversion • Service mindset

Rewards Strategy and Business Stage

	Startup	Growth	Mature	Decline
Salary	Low to mid	Mid to high	Mid to high	Mid to high (Freeze/cut)
Benefits	Low	Low	Mid to high	Mid to high
Short term incentives	Mid	High	High	High
Long term incentives	Nil to high	Nil to mid	Mid	Low to mid

6) Employer Branding with Signature Benefits

Benefits (especially unique perks) reflect the culture of the organization and differentiate the Employer brand. However, most companies adopt the "follow-the-herd" strategy of positioning all their employee benefits at market median! A firm without differentiated Benefits Strategy is like a ship that follows where the wind blows without any direction of its own. Benefits must be unique, meaningful, and set a company apart from their competitors. To stand-out from the herd, Companies should identify the "Signature benefits" that they want to be famous for. Get the newspapers to talk about it and brand the Signature benefits by giving them a quirky name.

According to Glassdoor, 57% of workers say that benefits are among the top things they consider when deciding whether to accept a job, and 80% of employees say that they would prefer new benefits, like health insurance or paid time off, over a pay raise. [1]

- Accenture: offers gender reassignment for its employees as part of its commitment to LGBTQ rights and diversity.
- Adobe: shuts down the company for one week in December and one week over the summer.
- Airbnb: gives its employees an annual stipend of $2,000 to travel and stay in an Airbnb listing anywhere in the world.
- Asana: employees have access to executive- and life-coaching services outside the company.
- Epic Systems Corp: offers employees a paid four-week sabbatical after five years at the company.
- Netflix: offers one paid year of maternity and paternity leave to new parents and allows parents to return part-time or full-time and take time off as needed throughout the year.
- PwC: offers its employees a $1,200-a-year reimbursement on student-loan debt.
- Salesforce: employees receive six days of paid volunteer time off a year, as well as $1,000 a year to donate to a charity of their choice.
- Twitter: provides on-site acupuncture.

- Walt Disney: offers employees and their friends and families free admission to its parks, and discounts on hotels and merchandise.
- Zillow: pays for overnight shipping of breast milk when a new mom is traveling.

References:

(1) Jacquelyn Smith, 17 incredible perks companies like Google, Facebook, and Airbnb offer their employees, https://www.businessinsider.sg/perks-companies-like-facebook-and-google-offer-their-employees-2016-9/?utm_content=buffer37238&utm_medium=social&utm_source=facebook.com&utm_campaign=buffer&r=US&IR=T&fbclid=IwAR0r1TMqcCCNuTvzLxSWXf95dQfZuL68i077BEiRLs0GuIYsRjNJRJHiapA (18 August 2019)

7) Flexi-benefits

Flexi-benefits are one of the solutions to address the diverse workforce needs. Although many employees rather get more pay than more benefits, others are desperate for time off or any help the company can give for their family issues. That's why companies are offering things such as flex time, work-from-home, and job-sharing. Compressed work week gives employees with dependents or employees talking part-time courses more flexibility in balancing work with their personal lives. The fundamental principles of Flexi-benefits address choice, flexibility and equity issues. Employees can tailor their benefits according to their individual needs. Singles with no dependants can use the "benefits credits" to fund their lifestyle instead of dependant medical coverage. Such employees appreciate Flexi-benefits due to a better fit between the benefits and their lifestyle needs especially as singles may feel they are subsidizing their colleagues with dependents. However, merely broadening the range of available benefits choice is not a strategy!

8) Factors influencing Benefits Globally

While remuneration tends to focus on the availability of internal and external data needed to make decisions, benefits tend to focus on the governmental, cultural and labour influences affecting program design. Although both remuneration and benefits are influenced by many factors, **the effect of external influences is arguably more pronounced in benefits** and hence warrants careful consideration on a country by country basis. Benefits involve variations in laws and regulations as well as in traditional practices in different parts of the world. Globally mobile employees may need a common point of reference to ensure equitable treatment with respect to vesting and compounding for time sensitive benefits. e.g. retirement benefits.

Various factors influence the growth and change of employee benefits:
- Labor Laws
- Industry practice
- Perceived value
- Costs
- Demographic changes
- Trade Blocs
- Tax laws

8.1) Labor Laws
In most countries, the government mandates or encourages employers to provide certain programs. In some countries, the government is the main provider of employee benefit programs. E.g. in Brunei, Bruneians & PRs are provided free medical at all Brunei Government Hospital & Clinic.

8.2) Industry practice
Employee benefits play a big role in helping the employer attract and retain the workforce it needs to carry out its mission.

8.3) Perceived value
Employees often request new or different benefits. Unions sometimes represent workers in negotiating with companies for benefits. Employers sometimes reconsider offering benefits that are not perceived by the workforce to be of value.

8.4) Costs
Rising employee benefits costs are a substantial issue in many countries. Demographic shifts in the workforce affect the cost of benefits programs and the demand for various work experience programs. Benefits plan design, deductibles and employee contributions may be adjusted to manage costs. In global regions that utilise service provider/vendors, selecting appropriate partners will have significant impact on costs.

8.5) Demographic changes
As the needs of a workforce change, employee benefits also need to change. E.g. Major additions to workforce, aging population in many countries (e.g. Thailand, China, Japan), increasing number of females in workforce.

8.6) Trade Blocs

There are several Trade blocs around the world. E.g. European union, North American Free Trade Agreement (NAFTA), Brazil, Argentina, Uruguay, and Latin America free trade area (Mercosur), Association of South East Asian Nations (ASEAN). Changes in multinational free trade areas affects employee benefits. The European Union has many protections for workers. UK has traditionally taken a minimalist approach to employment protection in line with the free-market philosophy that the market should not be restricted and the belief that competitive advantages promote good working practices. Without the EU being able to reinforce legislation, the opportunity to 'soften' or remove many pieces of legislation will become possible. For example,

- TUPE:– EU driven regulations protect the terms of employees who transfer employers under mergers, acquisitions and outsourcing indefinitely. The government may make it possible to harmonise terms and give employers more freedom when going through the process.

- Working time regulations:– Under EU, UK is subject to the weekly maximum hours, rest break and holiday entitlements. UK business are concern that such restrictions hinders businesses, damage their profitability, and make working environments too restrictive. But, removing this seems unlikely, as it would prove extremely unpopular to get rid of the voting public's right to a minimum of 5.6 weeks annual leave. However some aspects may be changed, such as limiting holiday pay to basic pay or removing the necessity to carry over annual leave for those who are on long-term sick leave.

- Discrimination:– the concepts of associative discrimination may be removed and a cap on compensation introduced.

- Agency workers regulations – These regulations give Agency workers in the UK the right to equal treatment as that of their permanent counterparts, and have a knock on effect for Recruitment Agencies looking to fill temporary agency positions. These unpopular rules may be abolished to give employers easier access to a flexible workforce.

8.7) Tax laws impacting benefits - Globally

Tax affects the provisions of benefits globally.

(i) Transport benefits tax – by Country

It is good to provide car benefits in China, Hong Kong, South Korea, and Taiwan because it is not taxable in these countries.

Country	Reimbursement of mileage	Transport allowance	Company owed car	Company rented car
Australia	Taxable	Taxable	Taxable	Taxable
China	Taxable	Taxable	Not taxable	Not taxable
Hong Kong	Taxable	Taxable	Not taxable	Not taxable
India	Not taxable	Taxable	Taxable	Taxable
Indonesia	Not taxable	Taxable	Taxable	Taxable
Japan	Not taxable	Not taxable up to JPY100,000 per month.	Taxable	Taxable
Malaysia	Not taxable	Not taxable to employees' annual transport allowance equal or less than RM2,400 per annum for travel between home & work place and/or RM6,000 per annum for travel on officials duties.	Taxable	Taxable
New Zealand	Not taxable	Not taxable if the employee is travelling to fulfill an obligation for the employer, or if there is no adequate public transport system serving the workplace.	Taxable	Taxable
Philippines	Not taxable	Not taxable to employee for PHP30,000 per year. The PHP30,000 limit includes 13th month pay plus other bonuses/	Taxable	Taxable

		allowances given to employees for the year, but exclude the over-time meal allowances and reimbursements		
Singapore	Not taxable	Taxable	Taxable	Taxable
South Korea	Not taxable	Not taxable for Car Allowance up to KRW 200,000 per month.	Not taxable	Not taxable
Taiwan	Not taxable to employee for mileage reimbursement rate below Taipei's taxi rate of THB20 per kilometer.	Taxable	Not taxable	Not taxable
Thailand	Not taxable	Taxable	Taxable	Taxable
Vietnam	Taxable	Taxable	Taxable	Taxable

1) AUSTRALIA

i) tax treatment on car & motorcycle mileage reimbursement claim: **taxable to employee.**

ii) tax treatment on transport allowance: **taxable to employee.**

iii) tax treatment on company car: **company car is considered as part of the salary package, hence it is taxable to employer for the employee private usage portion.**

iv) tax treatment on company rented car: **rented car is considered as residual fringe benefit to employee, taxable to employer.**

Source: http://www.exploroz.com/OntheRoad/FuelPrices/NSW.aspx

2) CHINA

i) tax treatment on car & motorcycle mileage reimbursement claim: **taxable to employee.**

ii) tax treatment on transport allowance: **taxable to employee.**

iii) tax treatment on company car: **where the employer provides use of a company car and driver however, these are exempt from tax.**

iv) tax treatment on company rented car: **company rented car is considered as expenses to company, not taxable to both employee and employer as it is for business use.**

China: http://oil.usd-cny.com/

3) HONG KONG
i) tax treatment on car & motorcycle mileage reimbursement claim: **taxable to employee.**
ii) tax treatment on transport allowance: **taxable to employee.**
iii) tax treatment on company car: **employees provided with company car for private purposes are free from tax liability, provided that employee does not convert the benefits into money.**
iv) tax treatment on company rented car: **company rented car paid by employer is considered as expenses to company, not taxable to employee.**
Source: http://www.shell.com/home/content/hongkong-en/news_and_library/press_releases/2009/price_adjust_petrol_diesel_20090818.html

4) INDIA
i) tax treatment on car & motorcycle mileage reimbursement claim: **not taxable to employee.**
ii) tax treatment on transport allowance: **taxable to employee for conveyance allowance exceeding RS 800 per month.**
iii) tax treatment on company car: **taxable to employee as it is considered a benefit.**
iv) tax treatment on company rented car: **taxable to employee as it is considered a benefit.**
Source: http://weeksupdate.com/2009/07/new-petroldiesel-price-india-new-delhi.html

5) INDONESIA

i) tax treatment on car & motorcycle mileage reimbursement claim: **not taxable to employee.**

ii) tax treatment on transport allowance: **taxable to employee.**

iii) tax treatment on company car: **company car designated to a particular employee that is taken home is taxable, payment of tax can be either employer or employee subject to agreement between both parties. However, company car for business purposes that is not designated and not taken home by any particular individual is not taxable to employer & employee, and the company must support with written memo that the car is for common use and to be returned to company after use.**

iv) tax treatment on company rented car: **company designated to a particular employee that is taken home is taxable, payment of tax can be either employer or employee subject to agreement between both parties. However, pool car for business purposes that is not designated and not taken home by any particular individual is tax deductible to employer as expenses and not taxable to employee. Company must support with written memo that the car is for common use and to be returned to company after use.**

Source:
http://www.bphmigas.go.id/p/bphmigaspages/bbm/daftar_harga_bbm.html

6) JAPAN

i) tax treatment on car & motorcycle mileage reimbursement claim: **not taxable to employee.**

ii) tax treatment on transport allowance:: **not taxable up to JPY100,000 per month.**

iii) tax treatment on company car: **private use of a company car is a taxable income to employee. However, company car for business purposes that is not designated and not taken home by any particular individual is not taxable to employee.**

iv) tax treatment on company rented car: **private use of a rented car is a taxable income to employee. However, pool car for business purposes that is not designated and not taken home by any particular individual is not taxable to employee.**

Source: http://oil-info.ieej.or.jp/price/price_ippan_kyuyujo_syuji.html

7) MALAYSIA

i) tax treatment on car & motorcycle mileage reimbursement claim: **not taxable to employee.**

ii) tax treatment on transport allowance: **Not taxable to employees' annual transport allowance equal or less than RM2,400 per annum for travel between home & work place and/or RM6,000 per annum for travel on officials duties.**

iii) tax treatment on company car: **taxable to employee and considered as benefits-in-kind.** However, company car for business purposes that is not designated and not taken home by any particular individual is not taxable to employer & employee. Company must support with written memo that the car is for common use and to be returned to company after use.

iv) tax treatment on company rented car: **taxable to employee and considered as benefits-in-kind.** However, pool car for business purposes is not designated and not taken home by any particular individual is tax deductible to employer as expenses and not taxable to employee, to support with written memo that it is for common use and to be returned to company after use.

Source: http://www.petrolmalaysia.com/

8) NEW ZEALAND

i) tax treatment on car & motorcycle mileage reimbursement claim: **not taxable.**

ii) tax treatment on transport allowance & car allowance: **Transport allowance & Car allowance is taxable to employee, if it is considered as Benefits allowances, and tax-free is if it is considered as Travelling allowances.** Definitions of Benefit allowances & Travelling allowances are as follows:

- Benefit allowances: Payments made in addition to salary or wages, which benefit the employee. A benefit allowance is taxed with the employee's wages in the pay period it is paid.
- Travelling allowances: It is tax-free if the amount paid reimburses an employee's additional transport costs and one or more of the following special circumstances exist:
    - ❖ the employee is working outside the normal hours of work (for example, overtime, shift or weekend work).
    - ❖ the employee needs to transport work-related tools and equipment - e.g. the employee normally takes the bus to work but has to use some other type of transport in order to carry work-related gear.
    - ❖ there is a temporary change in workplace.
    - ❖ the employee is travelling to fulfill an obligation for the employer.
    - ❖ there is some other condition of the employee's job.
    - ❖ there is no adequate public transport system serving the workplace. For all the special circumstances above, except the lack of adequate public transport, the tax free amount is the actual transport costs.

iii) tax treatment on company rented car: **taxable to employer, as it is considered as Fringe Benefit Tax.**

Source: http://www.aa.co.nz/motoring/owning/running-costs/petrolwatch/Pages/default.aspx

9) PHILIPPINES
i) tax treatment on car & motorcycle mileage reimbursement claim: **not taxable to employee.**

ii) tax treatment on transport allowance: **Not taxable to employee for PHP30,000 per year.** The PHP30,000 limit includes 13th month pay plus other bonuses/ allowances given to employees for the year, but exclude the over-time meal allowances and reimbursements.

iii) tax treatment on company car: **company car under company ownership is taxable to employer and considered as Fringe benefit tax.** However, company car for business purpose that is not designated and not taken home by any particular individual is not taxable to employer & employer. It must be defined in the company policy that the car is for all staff as a benefit for business purpose.

iv) tax treatment on company rented car: **taxable to employer and considered as Fringe benefit tax.** However, pool car for business purpose that is not designed and not taken home by any particular individual is tax deductible to employer as expenses and not taxable to employee. It must be defined in the company policy that the car is for all staff as a benefit for business purpose.

Source: http://www.doe.gov.ph/OPM/Archives.htm

10) SINGAPORE
i) tax treatment on car & motorcycle mileage reimbursement claim: **not taxable to employee.**

ii) tax treatment on transport allowance: **taxable to employee.**

iii) tax treatment on company car: **taxable to employee.** However, company car for business purpose that is not designated and not taken home by any particular individual is not taxable to employer & employer.

iv) tax treatment on company rented car: **taxable to employee.** However, pool car for business purposes that is not designated and not taken home by any particular individual is not taxable to employer and employee.

Source: http://www.petrolwatch.com.sg/

11) SOUTH KOREA

i) tax treatment on car & motorcycle mileage reimbursement claim: not taxable to employee.

ii) tax treatment on transport allowance: Not taxable for Car Allowance up to KRW200,000 per month.

iii) tax treatment on company car: for employees, a company car is tax free.

iv) tax treatment on company rented car: rented car is considered expenses to company, not taxable to employee.

Source: http://www.opinet.co.kr

12) TAIWAN

i) tax treatment on car & motorcycle mileage reimbursement claim: Not taxable to employee for mileage reimbursement rate below Taipei's taxi rate: initial fees THB70 for meter up to 1,250, thereafter THB5 for every increment of 250 meters (THB20 per kilometer).

ii) tax treatment on transport allowance: taxable to employee.

iii) tax treatment on company car: company car is considered company property for employee use, hence it is not taxable to employee & employer.

iv) tax treatment on company rented car: rented car under company name is taxable to employee as it is considered fringe income to employee and tax deductible to employer as expenses. However, pool car for business purpose that is not designated and not taken home by any particular individual is tax deductible to employer as expenses and not taxable to employee. Reimbursement of rental fees from company being car rental that is paid by the employee is tax free to employee, and has to be supported with document such as receipts that employee has paid.

Source: http://www.cpc.com.tw/big5_BD/tmtd/ListPrice/ShowListPrice_E.asp?pno=107&showtype=1

13) THAILAND
i) tax treatment on car & motorcycle mileage reimbursement claim: **not taxable to employee if reimbursement not via payroll.**
ii) tax treatment on transport allowance: **taxable to employee.**
iii) tax treatment on company car: **company car for use by a specific employee is taxable income to the employee. However, company car for business purposes that is not designated and not taken home by any particular individual is not taxable to employer & employee. It must be defined in the company policy that the car is for all staff as a benefit for business purpose.**
iv) tax treatment on company rented car: **rented car taxable income to employee. However, pool car for business purposes that is not designated and not taken home by any particular individual is tax deductible to employer as expenses and not taxable to employee, It must be defined in the company policy that the car is for all staff as a benefit for business purpose.**
Source: *http://www.pttplc.com/en/nc_oi.aspx*

14) VIETNAM
i) tax treatment on car & motorcycle mileage reimbursement claim: **taxable to employee.**
ii) tax treatment on transport allowance: **taxable to employee.**
iii) tax treatment on company car: **car and incidental costs are business-deductible expenses of the employer while these benefits may be taxable income of the employee.**
iv) tax treatment on company rented car: **rented car for employee usage will be taxable to employee as it is considered as benefit to employee.**
Source: *http://www.petrolimex.com.vn/Desktop.aspx/Home-En*

(ii) Meal benefits tax – by Country

It is good to provide meals benefits in Malaysia, Philippines, South Korea, Taiwan, and Vietnam, because it is not taxable in these countries.

Meal benefits tax

Country	Provision of Meal allowance
Malaysia	Not taxable
Philippines	Not taxable
Singapore	Taxable
South Korea	Not taxable for meal allowance below KRW100,000 per month
Taiwan	Not taxable to employee for both meal subsidy reimbursement claim and/or meal allowance equal to or less than TWD1,800 per month
Vietnam	Not taxable to employee for both meal subsidy reimbursement claim and/or meal allowance equal to or less than VND650,000 per month

Dated: 2009

(iii) Housing benefits tax – by Country

In certain countries there are tax savings to provide housing benefits.

Disclaimer: This Asia housing benefits tax guide is meant to be used as a quick general guide only and shall not be construed as advice, opinion, or recommendation.

Australia

Accommodation provided/reimbursed	Housing Allowance
Not taxable	Not taxable

Australia tax: http://www.ato.gov.au/individuals/content.asp?doc=/content/12333.htm&mnu=5053&mfp=001

Bangladesh

Accommodation provided/reimbursed	Housing Allowance
In Bangladesh, it is more tax effective structure the housing benefits as company provided accommodation. Accommodation provided to employee & expatriate is taxable for rental paid directly to owner of the accommodation. It is treated as an income assessed at the 'rental value' of such accommodation, OR 25% of the basic salary of the employee, whichever is less. Lease agreement must be under employer's name.	Not taxable to employee & expatriate for a maximum ceiling of BDT 15,000 per month or 50% of base salary, whichever is less.
Taxable to employee & expatriate for rental reimbursed to employee & expatriate, it is considered as housing allowance	

Bangladesh tax: http://www.asiatradehub.com/bangladesh/tax.asp

China

Accommodation provided/reimbursed	Housing Allowance
Taxable to employee	Taxable
Not taxable to expat for housing benefits if supported by receipts on reimbursement basis.	

China tax: http://www.chinatax.gov.cn/n480462/n480513/n480919/index.html

Hong Kong

Accommodation provided/reimbursed	Housing Allowance
In Hong Kong, it is more tax effective structure the housing benefits as company provided accommodation. Housing benefit is taxable to employee & expat based on the lesser of the rateable value of the premises (approximately the actual rental value) or a specified percentage of the assessable income of the employee (subject to certain adjustments). The specified percentages are as follows: • 4% — where the accommodation consists of not more than one room in a hotel, hostel or boarding-house. • 8% — where the accommodation consists of not more than two rooms in a hotel, hostel or boarding-house. • 10% — in all other cases except that the rateable value, as ascertained under the rating ordinance, may be substituted if smaller (sec 9(2)). Typical case of an employee renting a flat, the deemed housing benefit for the purposes of salaries tax will be 10% of his income, excluding certain items.	Taxable

Hong Kong tax: http://www.ird.gov.hk/eng/tax/ind_tra.htm#item03

India

Accommodation provided/reimbursed	Housing Allowance
In India, it is more tax effective structure the housing benefits as company provided accommodation, because only a portion (15% or 20%) of the income are subjected to tax instead of structuring the housing benefits as a cash allowance where 100% of the allowance is taxable in India. Employer-provided accommodation ("EPA") results in a perquisite in the hands of the employee. The perquisite value of EPA is determined at the lower of the following for the period during which EPA is provided, reduced by the amount recovered from the employee: • where the accommodation is owned by the employer: (a) 20% of salary, in a city having a population of more than 0.4 million, as per 2001 census; or (b) 15% of salary, in other cities; • where the accommodation is taken on lease or rented by the employer, lower of the: (a) actual amount of lease charges or rent paid; or (b) 20% of salary. Where furnished accommodation is provided, the perquisite value of EPA is increased by 10% of the cost of furniture per annum or actual hire charges payable, reduced by the amount recovered from the employee. Salary for the purpose of computing the perquisite value of EPA has been defined to include any pay, allowances, bonus or commission payable monthly or otherwise, or any monetary payment received from one or more employers, and excludes: • dearness allowance or dearness pay unless it is considered for retirement benefits;	Housing Rent Allowance (HRA) paid to an employee for meeting his expenditure towards hire of accommodation is exempt from tax up to the least of the following: • 50% of salary, where the house is situated in metro cities namely Delhi, Chennai, Kolkata and Mumbai and 40% of salary in other cases; • HRA received for the period for which rented accommodation is occupied by the employee; or • rent paid by the employee in excess of 10% of salary for the period for which rented

• employers' contribution to the provident fund; • allowances which are exempt from payment of tax; and • the value of other perquisites. Provision of hotel accommodation by the employer results in a perquisite in the hands of the employee. The perquisite value of hotel accommodation is determined at the lower of the following for the period during which accommodation is provided, reduced by the amount recovered from the employee: • actual charges paid or payable; or • 24% of salary paid or payable. No perquisite arises where hotel accommodation is provided for a period not exceeding 15 days in the aggregate, on the transfer of an employee. Salary has the same meaning as that for computation of perquisite value of EPA as discussed above. Dual accommodation Where an employee is provided accommodation at the place from where he is transferred and also at the place where he is relocated, no perquisite value arises for any one accommodation up to 90 days, and thereafter perquisite value arises for both the accommodations.	accommodation is occupied by the employee.

India tax: http://www.incometaxindia.gov.in/download_all.asp

Indonesia

Accommodation provided/reimbursed	Housing Allowance
Taxable for reimbursement of housing benefit.	Taxable
Not taxable to employee & expat, if accommodation rent/provided under employer's name.	

Indonesia tax: http://www.bkpm.go.id/

Japan

Accommodation provided/reimbursed	Housing Allowance
Where an employer leases a residence on behalf of its employees, the taxable benefit is calculated based on the tax base for property tax. Where an employer rents a residence on behalf of its directors, generally 50% of the rental costs is treated as the taxable benefit. If the residence is used for business purposes as well, the taxable benefit is reduced by 30%. Nonetheless, if the residence is considered as a luxury house, the full amount of rental costs is treated as the taxable benefit. Whether or not the residence is a luxury is determined by floor space (the general threshold is 240 square metres) and facilities. If the residence is small (less than a specified floor space), the taxable benefit is calculated in the same way as for an employee. Real estate tax - Property tax is imposed on certain fixed assets by the local government where the assets are located. Fixed assets subject to property tax are land, buildings and depreciable assets, excluding cars. The tax is payable by the individual who is registered as the owner of these fixed assets as of 1 January every year. The tax is levied at the rate of 1.4%. The tax base of land and buildings is revalued every 3 years by the local government and the tax base of depreciable assets is determined based on information returns submitted by the taxpayer every year. There are some concessionary measures to reduce the tax base for residential land and houses and also de minimis rules to exclude small assets. In addition to property tax,	Taxable

| local governments engaged in projects under the City Planning Act, etc. may impose city planning tax on land and buildings to obtain funds for such projects. The local government can determine the tax rate up to 0.3%. | |

Japan tax: http://www.nta.go.jp/foreign_language/index.htm

Malaysia

Accommodation provided/reimbursed	Housing Allowance
Housing accommodation provided by the employer is assessed at the lower of 30% of the employee's gross income or the defined value of the accommodation. Hotel accommodation is taxed at 3% of the employee's gross cash remuneration. From 1 January 2009, for the purposes of computing the taxable value of living/hotel accommodation, gross income excludes gross income in respect of an employee's right to acquire shares.	Taxable

Malaysia tax: http://www.hasil.gov.my/

Philippines

Accommodation provided/reimbursed	Housing Allowance
Not taxable to employee but taxable to employer as it is considered Fringe Benefit Tax	Not taxable to employee but taxable to employer as it is considered Fringe Benefit Tax

Philippines tax: http://www.bir.gov.ph/birforms/form_itr.htm

Singapore

Accommodation provided/reimbursed	Housing Allowance
Where employer provides the accommodation, the taxable benefit is the lower of 10% of employment income, or the annual value of the premises Less rent paid by employee (if any)	Taxable

Singapore tax: http://www.iras.gov.sg/irashome/default.aspx

South Korea

Accommodation provided/reimbursed	Housing Allowance
Not taxable to employee & expat, if accommodation rent/provided under employer's name.	Taxable

South Korea tax: http://www.nts.go.kr/eng

Taiwan

Accommodation provided/reimbursed	Housing Allowance
Not taxable to employee & expat, if lease agreement under employer's name (entity registered in Taiwan).	Taxable

Taiwan tax: http://investintaiwan.nat.gov.tw/

Thailand

Accommodation provided/reimbursed	Housing Allowance
Free accommodation provided by employer (Note: Department Instruction No. 23/2533); — if actual rent not known, 20% of salary/wages. — if known, based on actual rent, if the place is shared, allocated in proportion to the income of each person. - taxable to employee	Taxable

Thailand tax: http://www.rd.go.th/publish/6045.0.html

Vietnam

Accommodation provided/reimbursed	Housing Allowance
Taxable	Taxable

Vietnam tax: http://www.business.gov.vn/advice.aspx?id=2602

9) Categories of Benefits

Perquisites may be commonly provided in certain countries, for management positions, which may include company car, driver, enhanced insurance, club memberships, etc.

Benefits programs can be classified into two main categories:

(i) Income protection.
Income protection benefits are mean to protect the standard of living of the employee and their family. Income protection programs can be mandatory and non-mandatory. There are certain income protection benefits that are required by law, and certain benefits that employers offer by choice to accomplish organisational goals.
- **Healthcare benefits.** E.g. Medical, dental, vision, hearing
- **Welfare benefits.** E.g. Death benefits, Disability benefits
- **Retirement and investment plans.** Retirement benefits are provided by both government programs and company programs. Retirement plans may be classified as defined benefit (DB) or defined contribution (DC).

(ii) Pay for time not worked.
Pay for time not worked are designed to protect the employee's income flow during certain periods when the employee is not working, both "at work" and "not at work". E.g. annual leave, sick leave, maternity leave.
- **Pay for time not worked – at work.** E.g. Rest period, Wash up time, Clothes change time, Training and education, Travel time, Coffee and smoke breaks, Birthday celebrations, Department meetings
- **Pay for time not worked – not at work.** E.g. Vacations, Holidays, Personal leave, Sick leave, Bereavement, Company shutdown, Sabbatical, Military leave, Family/medical, Religious observations, Paid time off bank, Severance allowances.

9.1) Income Protection Plans

Income protection benefits are mean to protect the standard of living of the employee and their family. Main categories of Income protection benefits are: Healthcare benefits, Welfare benefits, Retirement and investment plans.

9.1.1) Healthcare benefits

Healthcare benefits can be provided by government and/or companies. Most countries have some form of government-mandated healthcare. Allocation of funding and resources will vary by country. Government-mandated healthcare programs may be referred to as social security or as other social programs. Employers commonly supplement government programs with healthcare plans aligned to corporate objectives, competitive practices and the limitations of government programs. Limitations of government-sponsored programs may include restricted access, limits on services or facilities, payments, reimbursement and gaps in coverage.

Some countries embrace alternative forms of healthcare such as Traditional Chinese Medicine (TCM) or hypnotherapy, and it may be effective and may be less expensive than western medical care for certain conditions.

Companies globally are concerned with the rising cost of healthcare. Because of the rising cost of providing medical benefits, private medical plans have evolved into a more "managed care" environment.

Most small businesses think that their new annual healthcare insurance premium cannot be negotiated. However, small businesses often have more leverage than they think. Health insurers will usually justifying reasons to increase the small company's premiums by saying that all the company's employees are a year older, or that the company has a few of large claims. To gain leverage, companies can highlight factors that the insurer should also consider to lower the premium. For example, some older claimants have left the company, or the medical cost is decreasing in the last few months.

Claims ratio is the ratio of the net claim settled by the insurer to the net premiums collected in a year. This is the equivalent of gross profit margin for an insurance business. The formula for claims ratio is:

Claims ratio = Claims paid / Billed Premium

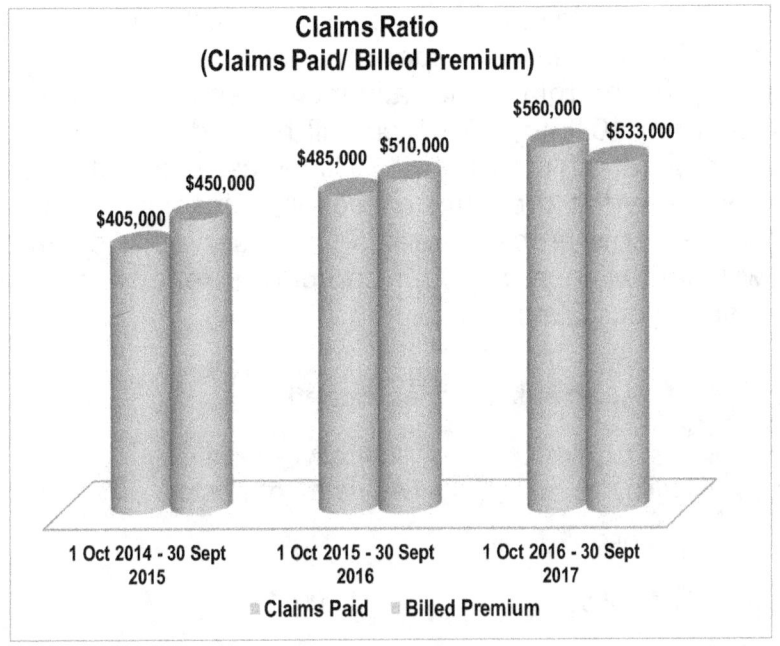

	Year 2015	Year 2016	Year 2017
Medical Paid	$405,000	$485,000	$560,000
Billed Premium	$450,000	$510,000	$533,000
Claims Ratio	**90%** ($405,000/ $450,000)	**95%** ($485,000/ $510,000)	**105%** ($560,000/ $533,000)

From the insurer's perspective, a higher claims ratio means lower profits for them, because a 90% claims ratio means that 90% of the premiums collected or earned in the year are spent for claim settlements and the balance 10% is the profit margin. If the ratio increases to 95%, the profit of the insurer will fall from 10% to 5% which will be bad from the Insurer's revenue experience. A ratio higher than 100% indicates that the Insurer is incurring losses because the premium collection is insufficient to pay the claims and so the insurer is probably utilizing its reserves to settle claims. Thus, Insurers will want to increase your company's renewal premiums if there is an increase in your Claims Ratio.

Medical Insurance Benefits	
Annualized Loss Ratio	Illustrative Premium Adjustment Factor
<= 65.0%	0%
65.1% to 85%	Up to 31%
85.1% to 90%	Up to 39%
90.1% to 95%	Up to 47%
> 95%	> 47%

Claims paid is a lagging key performance indicator (KPI). Most financial indicators such as revenue, profit, costs are "lacking indicators". Lagging indicators as the name indicates, are lagging, and this means you are analyzing behaviors and results that have already taken place, and can't be changed. To improve employee health and slash your company's wasteful healthcare spending with predictive analytics, you will need to track leading KPIs as they are predictive in nature.

	Lagging KPI	Leading KPI		
	2017 KPI	Q1	Q2	Q3
Average Outpatient Doctor visits	6.0	1.5	1.6	1.4
Average Outpatient Doctor bill size	$34	25	26	$27
Specialist referral	Less than 10%	1%	1%	1%

Listed below are several design components utilised when establishing and renewing medical plans.

Medical plans.
- **Deductible.** Typically, an amount paid up front by the member for services rendered.
- **Co-insurance.** The percentage paid by member and plan after the deductible has been met.
- **Co-payment.** The total dollar amount that the member pays for covered services rendered at the time of service.
- **Usual, customary and reasonable charges.** The charges that an insurance carrier determines are normal for a particular medical procedure within a specific geographical area.
- **Out of packet maximum.** The total dollar amount limit that the member will be liable for in relation to the co-insurance.
- **Coordination of benefits.** Helps ensure that the correct medical plan is paying expenses when a member is covered under more than one plan. E.g. an employee is covered under his or her plan and also under a spouse's plan.

Dental plans.
Indemnity plans cover preventive and limited basic and major care. Dental maintenance organisation plans require use of participating providers.

Vision plans.
Insured plans with periodic coverage of routine exam, lenses and frames. Discount plans with retail networks.

Hearing plans.
Plans with coverage for routine exams and hearing aids. Discounts with network providers.

9.1.2) Welfare benefits

Death benefits.
Company provided death benefits are prevalent in most countries.
- Benefits vary in both form and amount.
- Not always or commonly insured.
- May be offered in some countries as a social program; human resources should examine benefits available in each country to avoid over-insuring employees. E.g. Italy is among the countries with the highest benefits (five to six times of pay).
- Payout relative to annual salary; one to two times pay is common; fixed amount in some countries, regardless of salary.
- Payout options: Lump sum or instalment/annuity.

Disability benefits.
Also known globally as long-term disability, invalidity, or permanent ill health. Similar provisions of death benefits; payments may be minor or substantial. not yet provided in some countries. Determination and definition of disability will differ. Payments often on a scheduled basis and range from 30% to 100% of pay. Typically limited to base pay. Local workers' compensation may provide benefits for work related disability.

9.1.3) Retirement and Investment Plans

Retirement benefits are provided by both government programs and company programs. In some countries, retirement programs are quite substantial. In others, they may be virtually non-existent. Programs may be influenced by local collective agreements. Retirement plans may be classified as defined benefit (DB) or defined contribution (DC).

9.1.4) Defined benefit (DB) plans

"Defined benefit". A defined benefit plan guarantees a certain payout at retirement, according to a fixed formula. The formula that can incorporate the employee's pay, years of employment, age at retirement, and other factors. What you get at retirement does not match how much you contributed. Government pensions such as Social Security in the United States are a type of defined benefit pension plan. A defined benefit plan places the financial risk on the employer. An employer commits to paying an employee a predetermined amount at the time of their retirement for life, either as a percentage of salary annually, or as a set dollar amount per pay period. An employee usually has to remain employed for a certain period of time before they are eligible for retirement benefits (known as a vesting period). Once an employee is vested, they are eligible to receive retirement benefits upon reaching a retirement age even if they change jobs, making it possible to qualify for multiple retirements benefits. This poses a risk for employers that have no guarantee that the amounts contributed by the employee or employer will be enough to cover retiree benefits. If investment performance or age of retirees exhaust the pension fund, the employer is still responsible for covering benefits.

9.1.5) Defined contribution (DC) plans worldwide

"Defined contribution" means how much you get at retirement depends on how much you contributed and how much your money earned. A defined contribution plan will provide a payout at retirement that is dependent upon the amount of money contributed and the performance of the investment vehicles utilized. In a defined contribution plan the employee bears the financial risk. If the investment return on the retirement savings is weak or the employee lives longer than planned, the employee risks not having enough income to survive through retirement.

Some countries may provide richer benefits through government/social security programmes, reducing the need for company-sponsored voluntary benefits.

Countries with Defined Contribution (DC) Plans

"Defined contribution" means how much you get at retirement depends on how much you contributed and how much your money earned. A defined contribution plan will provide a payout at retirement that is dependent upon the amount of money contributed and the performance of the investment vehicles utilized.

Countries	Details
India	All Government and Private sector organizations has to offer Provident Fund (PF), a type of Defined Contribution Plan. Earlier employees were under Defined Benefit Plan. The Provident Fund (PF) authority choose the investment vehicle, however the beneficiaries are given a standard % of returns on their contribution.
Japan	Defined contribution schemes existed in Japan since year 2001.
Singapore	The Central Provident Fund (CPF) is Singapore's national pension fund. Depending on their age group, employers contribute up to 17% per month, while employees contribute up to 20% per month of their salary.
United Kingdom	Most employers have moved from defined benefit schemes to defined contribution, where the employer makes regular payments (usually a percentage of salary) into a pension fund, and the fund is used to buy a pension when the employee retires.
United States	Examples of defined contribution plans in the US include Individual Retirement Accounts (IRAs) and 401(k) plans. The employee is responsible for selecting the types of investments which the funds in the retirement plan are allocated. Most defined contribution plans have tax advantages, with a portion of the employee's contributions matched by the employer. The funds in these plans may not be withdrawn by the employee prior to reaching a certain age.

Dated: 2019

Hybrid plans combine elements of DB and DC plans.
E.g. cash balance plans, pension equity.

Company programs.
Company sponsored retirement programs present challenges in both the determination of appropriate benefit levels and alignment with local practices. Some government programs may reduce benefits when coverage is provided by company plans. Company plan design should consider eligibility for social security and other mandatory benefits, the effect of other governmental restrictions (e.g. tax treatment), competitive practices, union, cost and business need. Defined benefit, defined contribution and hybrid programs (i.e. cash balance, pension equity) are all used globally. For example, defined contribution is popular in countries with a British influence and defined benefit plans are found in parts of Europe and the Americas.

9.2) Pay for time not worked

Paid time off – time off with pay is provided for a variety of situations in different countries and refers to any nonworking period for which the regular rate of pay is earned.

Pay for time not worked – at work
- Rest period
- Wash up time
- Clothes change time
- Training and education
- Travel time
- Coffee and smoke breaks
- Birthday celebrations
- Department meetings

Pay for time not worked – not at work
- Vacations
- Personal leave
- Sick leave
- Bereavement
- Company shutdown
- Sabbatical
- Military leave
- Family/medical
- Religious observations
- Paid time off bank.
  Collapses separate programs into one policy. It replaces what are traditionally segregated time off programs into a single block of time. Combines vacation, sick, personal days and sometimes holidays into one-time off bank.
- Severance allowances.
  A continuation of an employee's salary after termination that is paid either in a lump sum or on a continuation basis.
- Public holidays.
  Countries with greater religious diversity may have more paid public holidays.

Annual leave legislation worldwide

Annual Leave

Countries	Statutory	Labour Law provision
Australia	4 weeks	4 weeks for each year of service
Brazil	30 days	30 days
China	7 – 15 days	7 – 15 days depending on length of service
India	12 days	1 day for every 20 days' work, which is around 12 days a year.
France	30 calendar days	The law provides five weeks of paid vacation (30 calendar days plus Sundays).
Germany	20 – 24 days	24 working days for a six-day week. 20 working days for a six-day week.
Singapore	7 – 14 days	7 – 14 days depending on length of service
South Africa	21 days	21 consecutive calendar days' paid leave per year
South Korea	15 – 25 days	15 to 25 days depending on years of service
United Arab Emirates	30 days	30 days in a year if service more than 1 year
United Kingdom	28 days	28 working days of annual leave each year.
United States	NA	Federal law does not require employers to provide vacation benefits.

Dated: 2015

Sick leave legislation worldwide

Sick Leave

Countries	Statutory	Labour Law provision
Australia	10 days	10 days' paid personal leave per year
Brazil	15 days	15 days at full pay
China	3 – 24 months	3 to 24 months depending on years in the company.
India	10 days	Each state has its own regulations for sick leave. Average number of such leave days provided by state regulations is 10 days per year.
France	unlimited	The law provide for paid absence due to illness. There is no annual limit of the number of days off due to illness.
Germany	6 weeks	After three days of illness, employees must present a medical certificate. Employers pay salary for the first six weeks.
Singapore	14 days	14 days at full pay, extended to 60 days if hospitalized
South Africa	6 weeks	Six weeks
South Korea	NA	no provision for this benefit
United Arab Emirates	90 days	90 days' sick leave for every year of service. First 15 days at full pay, next 30 days at half pay, next 45 days at no pay
United Kingdom	28 weeks	up to 28 weeks statutory sick pay
United States	NA	no federal provision

Dated: 2015

Maternity leave legislation worldwide

Maternity Leave

Countries	Statutory	Labour Law provision
Australia	13 weeks	Payments may be payable up to 13 weeks
Brazil	120 days	120 continuous days
China	98 day	98 days' paid leave after childbirth
India	12 weeks	The maximum benefit period is 12 weeks
France	16 to 26 weeks	The law provide for maternity leave of 16 to 26 weeks, depending on the number of current children and if it is a multiple birth.
Germany	14 weeks	The leave entitlement for mothers is six weeks before and eight weeks after the birth.
Singapore	16 weeks	16 weeks
South Africa	4 months	Maternity leave entitlement is four months
South Korea	90 days	An employer must provide 90 days' paid leave
United Arab Emirates	45 days	45 days full pay if worked with employer for more than 1 year
United Kingdom	52 weeks	52 weeks' maternity leave irrespective of length of service or hours worked.
United States	12 weeks	12 weeks of unpaid leave annually

Dated: 2015

10) How to read employees benefits survey reports

What to look for in Benefits surveys
- Participating companies
- Sample size
- Geographic representation
- Value (Quality, Cost, Timelines)
- Confidentiality
- Service Quality

Survey Report Example 1: Leave Benefits

Typical Benefits Report Information: Annual Leave

Basic annual leave entitlement (number of days)

	Lower Decile	Lower Quartile	Median	Upper Quartile	Upper Decile	Average
Top Management	15	20	21	24	28	22
Senior Management	15	17	20	22	25	20
Middle Management	14	16	19	22	24	19
Professional/ Supervisory	14	15	18	21	24	18
Support	12	14	14	16	19	15

Survey Report Example 2: Car Benefits

Typical Benefits Report Information: Car Allowance

Car allowance (USD'000 per year)

	Lower Decile	Lower Quartile	Median	Upper Quartile	Upper Decile	Average
Top Management	4	7	35	50	85	35
Senior Management	3	10	35	38	50	30
Middle Management	4	6	12	25	25	20
Professional/ Supervisory	5	7	10	26	35	15
Support	-	-	6	-	-	5

Survey Report Example 3: Life and Disability Insurance

Typical Benefits Report Information: Life Insurance

Do companies provide life insurance benefits in addition to statutory coverage?

	Percentage of Organizations
Yes	85%
No	15%

Life insurance benefits – fixed multiple of monthly salary

	25th Percentile	Average	Median	75th Percentile	No. of Responses
Executives	24	31	36	36	510
Management	24	30	30	36	520
Professional	24	29	26	36	500
Para--Professional	24	28	24	36	480

Survey Report Example 4: Clinical Care Coverage

Typical Benefits Report Information: Clinical Care Coverage

Company paid clinical coverage (average amount)

Coverage type	Top Management	Senior Management	Middle Management	Professional	Support Staff
Outpatient visit (USD per visit)	38	38	38	38	38
Outpatient specialist (USD per annum)	1300	1150	1050	1030	900

11) Employees benefits reports - Globally

(i) Housing allowance - by Country

This section shows the housing allowance per month (US$) by countries.

Housing allowance per month (US$) – by Country

		India	Japan	Australia	South Korea	Singapore	Taiwan	Malaysia
Min	Company Head	8200	8000	5119	4487	2601	3243	1714
	Function Head	-	-	-	-	2384	2625	1551
	Manager	-	-	-	-	1806	-	1359
	Non-Manager	-	-	-	-	1445	-	1005
	Overall	8200	8000	5119	4487	1445	2625	1005
Median	Company Head	8200	8000	5119	4944	4335	3243	1825
	Function Head	-	-	-	-	3396	1000	1670
	Manager	-	-	-	-	2890	-	1389
	Non-Manager	-	-	-	-	2168	-	1019
	Overall	8200	8000	5119	4944	3251	2934	1640
Max	Company Head	10000	8000	5119	5400	14450	3243	1921
	Function Head	-	-	-	-	8670	2625	1773
	Manager	-	-	-	-	8670	-	1389
	Non-Manager	-	-	-	-	4335	-	1019
	Overall	10000	8000	5119	5400	14450	3243	1921
	Sample size	1	1	1	2	16	1	2

Notes:
- *Source: Cedric Ng Mong Shen (2009) Asia housing benefits survey report, 2019 September 8*
- *This survey report shows the employee housing benefits market practice for 13 countries in Asia.*
- *Market data for countries/cities with less than 3 sample size may not be reflective of the median market practice.*
- *Figures in this table include individuals, with spouse, and with child.*

Housing allowance per month (US$) – by Country

		Hong Kong	China	Philippines	Thailand	Indonesia	Vietnam
Min	Company Head	1419	732	1000	753	800	721
	Function Head	1419	723	1000	542	578	649
	Manager	1419	439	1000	800	800	649
	Non-Manager	-	293	1000	800	800	505
	Overall	1419	293	1000	542	578	505
Median	Company Head	1419	1245	1200	1000	1000	1000
	Function Head	1419	1000	1200	852	1000	938
	Manager	1419	513	1200	1000	1000	1000
	Non-Manager	-	366	1200	1000	1000	1000
	Overall	1419	1245	1200	1000	1000	1000
Max	Company Head	1419	10691	1200	3267	1445	3000
	Function Head	10709	8787	1200	1506	1156	2000
	Manager	1419	6005	1200	1000	1000	1000
	Non-Manager	-	3496	1200	1000	1000	1000
	Overall	10709	10691	1200	3267	1445	3000
	Sample size	2	11	1	3	2	6

Notes:
- *Source: Cedric Ng Mong Shen (2009) Asia housing benefits survey report, 2019 September 8.*
- *This survey report shows the employee housing benefits market practice for 13 countries in Asia.*
- *Market data for countries/cities with less than 3 sample size may not be reflective of the median market practice.*
- *Figures in this table include individuals, with spouse, and with child.*

(ii) Housing rental prices - by Country

This section shows the list of housing rental websites worldwide. Other than market practice, the actual cost of housing rental can also be used to derive the expatriate housing allowance quantum for various countries worldwide.

1) Australia
- http://www.sublet.com/spider/lesearch.asp?state=australia

2) Bangladesh
- http://www.rehabhousing.com/

3) Brazil
- http://www.vivareal.net/buy/brazil/brasilia/

4) Britain
- http://www.upad.co.uk/

5) China
- http://world.soufun.com/
- http://www.servicedapartmentschina.com/index.aspx
- http://www.newportchina.com/

6) UAE (Dubai)
- http://www.dubaiproperties.ae/main/find_dubai_properties/?cboPage=1&cboListingMode=Rent&cboPropType=0&cboCommunity=0&cboBedRoom=0
- http://www.durentals.me/Residential.html
- http://www.dubairentalproperties.co.uk/Page.aspx?name=About_Us
- http://www.property-dubai.tv/0/properties/?category=Residential+-+Rental&country=UAE&location=Dubai&province=&price=&search=search

7) France
- http://www.immostreet.co.uk/annonces.htm?lang=en&idpays=250&idtt=1&aidecp=1&region=20&cp=13
- http://www.immostreet.co.uk/annonces.htm?lang=en&idpays=250&idtt=1&aidecp=1&region=10&cp=92
- http://www.arkadia.com/usa/real-estate/for-rent/france/ile-de-france/hauts-de-seine/meudon/
- http://www.arkadia.com/usa/real-estate/for-rent/france/provence-alpes-cote-d-azur/bouches-du-rhone/la-ciotat/
- http://www.arkadia.com/usa/real-estate/for-rent/france/provence-alpes-cote-d-azur/bouches-du-rhone/gemenos/
- http://www.rentcom.info/rentalsparis/rental-paris.html

8) Germany
- http://www.arkadia.com/usa/real-estate/for-rent/germany/baden-wurttemberg/stuttgart/filderstadt/

9) Hong Kong
- http://qi-homes.com/en/index.php
- http://www.expatflats.com/hong-kong-apartment-rentals.html
- http://www.gohome.com.hk/english/home.asp
- http://islandproperty.com.hk/rent.php
- http://www.hongkonghomes.com/property_search/form.php?sch_type=1&location=64&pr_from=0&pr_to=100000000&rt_from=0&rt_to=180000&keywords=&page=1&rec_per_page=5&sort_by=3&action=1&mode=1&max_page=0

10) India
- http://in.iproperty.com/
- http://www.99acres.com/
- http://www.bharathrentals.com/browse/Available/all/all

11) Indonesia
- http://www.sublet.com/spider/lesearch.asp?country=13

12) Japan
- http://www.sakura-house.com/english/search.php
- http://www.jafnet.co.jp/plus/month_top/company_list_e.php?id=3
- http://www.jafnet.co.jp/plaza/contentse/e_top.htm

13) Malaysia
- http://www.sublet.com/spider/lesearch.asp?country=13
- http://www.iproperty.com.my/

14) New Zealand
- http://www.apartments.co.nz/

15) Philippines
- http://www.islandsproperties.com/rentals/1makati.htm
- http://www.sublet.com/spider/lesearch.asp?country=13
- http://www.iproperty.com.ph/

16) Singapore
- http://www.singaporeexpats.com/housing-in-singapore/search/singapore-apartment-rent.htm
- http://www.hdb.gov.sg/fi10/fi10206p.nsf/WPDis/Subletting%20Your%20Flat%20/%20RoomStatistics-%20Median%20Subletting%20Rents%20by%20Town%20and%20Flat%20Type?OpenDocument#
- http://www.propertyguru.com.sg/
- http://singapore.roomsdb.net/display_offers.php
- http://www.homebiznez.com/info/guide_aptrent1.htm
- http://www.moveandstay.com/singapore/servicedapartments.asp
- http://www.iproperty.com.sg/property/searchresult.aspx?t=R&gpt=P&pt=CO&ds=&mp=0&xp=500000000&k=&mbr=0&xbr=9&mbu=0&xbu=999999&rmp=10&sby=wpz
- http://www.nationproperty.sg/
- http://www.singaporecondo.com/
- http://property.st701.com/

17) South Korea
- http://www.korearent.kr/search/index.asp?find=find
- http://www.nicerent.com/mn_seoul_real_estate_advenced/advenced_main_frm.asp

18) Taiwan
- http://taipei.sublet.com/
- http://www.vrhouse.com.tw/

19) Thailand
- http://www.ahomefinder.net/property_for_rent.php
- http://www.servicedapartmentsasia.com/propertylisting.aspx?Country=6&City=Bangkok
- http://www.sublet.com/spider/lesearch.asp?country=13

20) USA
- http://www.findhomerentals.com/home_rental/search.asp

21) Vietnam
- http://www.hanoihousehunter.com/index.php?hho=type&type=rent
- http://www.sublet.com/spider/lesearch.asp?country=13

(iii) Car mileage claim rate – by Country

Car mileage claim rates should not be the same for different countries because different countries have different petrol prices and market practices. However, car mileage claims rates can be set globally, if you have the market Car mileage claim rates for various countries.

Prevalence of car reimbursement of mileage

Country	Sample size	Companies providing	% of companies providing
Australia	10 companies	5 companies	50%
China	12 companies	6 companies	50%
Hong Kong	10 companies	3 companies	30%
India	10 companies	4 companies	40%
Indonesia	8 companies	2 companies	25%
Japan	5 companies	2 companies	40%
Malaysia	19 companies	16 companies	84%
New Zealand	1 company	1 company	100%
Philippines	6 companies	2 companies	33%
Singapore	41 companies	37 companies	90%
South Korea	6 companies	3 companies	50%
Taiwan	7 companies	3 companies	43%
Thailand	13 companies	6 companies	46%
Vietnam	7 companies	2 companies	29%
	155 companies	92 companies	51%

Source: Cedric Ng Mong Shen (2009) Asia-Pacific Mileage Claim Survey Report, 2019 September 8.

Car reimbursement of mileage amount

Country	Sample size (no. of companies)	(US$ per km)				
		Min	Lower quartile	Median	Upper quartile	Max
Australia	5 companies	US$0.59	US$0.59	US$0.60	US$0.61	US$0.62
China	6 companies	US$0.15	US$0.15	US$0.20	US$0.29	US$0.31
Hong Kong	3 companies	US$0.25	US$0.26	US$0.27	US$0.27	US$0.27
India	4 companies	US$0.12	US$0.15	US$0.19	US$0.21	US$0.21
Indonesia	2 companies	US$0.11	US$0.14	US$0.17	US$0.20	US$0.22
Japan	2 companies	US$0.37	US$0.40	US$0.43	US$0.45	US$0.48
Malaysia	16 companies	US$0.14	US$0.16	US$0.17	US$0.20	US$0.23
New Zealand	1 company	-	-	US$0.46	-	-
Philippines	2 companies	US$0.12	US$0.15	US$0.17	US$0.19	US$0.22
Singapore	37 companies	US$0.10	US$0.35	US$0.42	US$0.45	US$0.56
South Korea	3 companies	US$0.20	US$0.25	US$0.30	US$0.30	US$0.30
Taiwan	3 companies	US$0.24	US$0.24	US$0.24	US$0.27	US$0.30
Thailand	6 companies	US$0.12	US$0.13	US$0.16	US$0.18	US$0.23
Vietnam	2 companies	US$0.12	US$0.12	US$0.12	US$0.12	US$0.12

Source: Cedric Ng Mong Shen (2009) Asia-Pacific Mileage Claim Survey Report, 2019 September 8.

Car reimbursement of mileage amount

Country	Sample size (no. of companies)	(Local currency per km)				
		Min	Lower quartile	Median	Upper quartile	Max
Australia	5 companies	AUD0.70	AUD0.70	AUD0.72	AUD0.74	AUD0.80
China	6 companies	RMB1.00	RMB1.00	RMB1.34	RMB1.99	RMB2.10
Hong Kong	3 companies	HKD1.90	HKD2.00	HKD2.10	HKD2.10	HKD2.10
India	4 companies	INR6.00	INR7.50	INR9.00	INR10.00	INR10.00
Indonesia	2 companies	IDR1,150	IDR1,425	IDR1,700	IDR1,975	IDR2,250
Japan	2 companies	JPY35.00	JPY37.50	JPY40.00	JPY42.50	JPY45.00
Malaysia	16 companies	MYR0.50	MYR0.55	MYR0.60	MYR0.70	MYR0.80
New Zealand	1 company	-	-	NZD0.67	-	-
Philippines	2 companies	PHP6.00	PHP7.15	PHP8.30	PHP9.45	PHP10.6
Singapore	37 companies	SGD0.14	SGD0.50	SGD0.60	SGD0.65	SGD0.80
South Korea	3 companies	KRW250	KRW315	KRW380	KRW390	KRW400
Taiwan	3 companies	TWD8.00	TWD8.00	TWD8.00	TWD9.00	TWD10.00
Thailand	6 companies	THB4.00	THB4.30	THB5.60	THB6.00	THB8.00
Vietnam	2 companies	VND2,137	VND2,137	VND2,137	VND2,137	VND2,137

Source: Cedric Ng Mong Shen (2009) Asia-Pacific Mileage Claim Survey Report, 2019 September 8.

(iv) Motorcycle mileage claim rate – by Country

Motorcycle mileage claim rates should not be the same for different countries because different countries have different petrol prices and market practices. However, car mileage claims rates can be set globally, if you have the market Motorcycle mileage claim rates for various countries.

Prevalence of motorcycle reimbursement of mileage

Country	Sample size	Companies providing	% of companies providing
Australia	10 companies	1 company	10%
China	12 companies	1 company	8%
Hong Kong	10 companies	2 companies	20%
India	10 companies	3 companies	30%
Indonesia	8 companies	2 companies	25%
Japan	5 companies	2 companies	40%
Malaysia	19 companies	8 companies	42%
New Zealand	1 company	0 company	0%
Philippines	6 companies	1 company	17%
Singapore	41 companies	26 companies	63%
South Korea	6 companies	1 company	17%
Taiwan	7 companies	1 company	14%
Thailand	13 companies	3 companies	23%
Vietnam	7 companies	1 company	14%
	155 companies	52 companies	23%

Source: Cedric Ng Mong Shen (2009) Asia-Pacific Mileage Claim Survey Report, 2019 September 8.

Motorcycle reimbursement of mileage amount

Country	Sample size (no. of companies)	Min (US$ per km)	Lower quartile	Median	Upper quartile	Max
Australia	1 company	-	-	US$0.25	-	-
China	1 company	-	-	US$0.10	-	-
Hong Kong	2 companies	US$0.10	US$0.11	US$0.11	US$0.11	US$0.11
India	3 companies	US$0.08	US$0.09	US$0.10	US$0.11	US$0.12
Indonesia	2 companies	US$0.03	US$0.03	US$0.03	US$0.03	US$0.03
Japan	2 companies	US$0.16	US$0.17	US$0.18	US$0.19	US$0.20
Malaysia	8 companies	US$0.04	US$0.10	US$0.11	US$0.14	US$0.18
New Zealand	0 company	-	-	-	-	-
Philippines	1 company	-	-	US$0.09	-	-
Singapore	26 companies	US$0.07	US$0.14	US$0.17	US$0.21	US$0.45
South Korea	1 company	US$0.08	US$0.08	US$0.08	US$0.08	US$0.08
Taiwan	1 company	-	-	US$0.11	-	-
Thailand	3 companies	US$0.04	US$0.08	US$0.12	US$0.12	US$0.12
Vietnam	1 company	-	-	US$0.05	-	-

Source: Cedric Ng Mong Shen (2009) Asia-Pacific Mileage Claim Survey Report, 2019 September 8.

Motorcycle reimbursement of mileage amount

Country	Sample size (no. of companies)	(Local currency per km)				
		Min	Lower quartile	Median	Upper quartile	Max
Australia	1 company	-	-	AUD0.30	-	-
China	1 company	-	-	RMB0.70	-	-
Hong Kong	2 companies	HKD0.80	HKD0.82	HKD0.84	HKD0.86	HKD0.88
India	3 companies	INR3.80	INR4.40	INR5.00	INR5.50	INR6.00
Indonesia	2 companies	IDR325	IDR325	IDR325	IDR325	IDR325
Japan	2 companies	JPY14.70	JPY15.75	JPY16.80	JPY17.85	JPY18.90
Malaysia	8 companies	MYR0.15	MYR0.36	MYR0.40	MYR0.50	MYR0.65
New Zealand	0 company	-	-	-	-	-
Philippines	1 company	-	-	PHP4.45	-	-
Singapore	26 companies	SGD0.10	SGD0.20	SGD0.25	SGD0.30	SGD0.65
South Korea	1 company	KRW105	KRW105	KRW105	KRW105	KRW105
Taiwan	1 company	-	-	TWD3.50	-	-
Thailand	3 companies	THB1.50	THB2.75	THB4.00	THB4.00	THB4.00
Vietnam	1 company	-	-	VND898	-	-

Source: Cedric Ng Mong Shen (2009) Asia-Pacific Mileage Claim Survey Report, 2019 September 8.

(v) Petrol prices – by Country

This section shows the petrol prices of Asia-Pacific countries. Other than market practice, petrol prices can be used as a basis to derive the mileage claim rate for various countries. Among the Asia-Pacific countries in this study, South Korea petrol prices are the highest, whereas Malaysia petrol prices are the lowest.

Country	Petrol Price		Median Car mileage claim	
	(US$/ Litre)	(Local currency/ Litre)	(US$/ km)	(Local currency/ km)
South Korea	US$1.95/Litre	KRW2428/Litre	US$0.30/km	KRW380/km
Japan	US$1.37/Litre	JPY125/Litre	US$0.43/km	JPY40.00/km
Singapore	US$1.22/Litre	SGD1.8/Litre	US$0.42/km	SGD0.60/km
Taiwan	US$1.05/Litre	TWD35/Litre	US$0.24/km	TWD8.00/km
Thailand	US$1.05/Litre	THB35/Litre	US$0.16/km	THB5.60/km
Hong Kong	US$1.01/Litre	HKD7.8/Litre	US$0.27/km	HKD2.10/km
Australia	US$1.00/Litre	AUD1.2/Litre	US$0.60/km	AUD0.72/km
India	US$1.00/Litre	INR49/Litre	US$0.19/km	INR9.00/km
Vietnam	US$0.85/Litre	VND15,138/Litre	US$0.12/km	VND2,137/km
China	US$0.81/Litre	CNY5.5/Litre	US$0.20/km	RMB1.34/km
New Zealand	US$0.80/Litre	NZD1.17/Litre	US$0.46/km	NZD0.67/km
Philippines	US$0.78/Litre	PHP38/Litre	US$0.17/km	PHP8.30/km
Indonesia	US$0.59/Litre	IDR5,959/Litre	US$0.17/km	IDR1,700/km
Malaysia	US$0.50/Litre	MYR1.8/Litre	US$0.17/km	MYR0.60/km

Source: Cedric Ng Mong Shen (2009) Asia-Pacific Mileage Claim Survey Report, 2019 September 8.

The Petrol prices were collected from the following websites in August 2009. To get the updated petrol prices, you can visit these sites:
- **Australia:** http://www.exploroz.com/OntheRoad/FuelPrices/NSW.aspx
- **China:** http://oil.usd-cny.com/
- **Hong Kong:** http://www.shell.com/home/content/hongkong-en/news_and_library/press_releases/2009/price_adjust_petrol_diesel_20090818.html
- **India:** http://weeksupdate.com/2009/07/new-petroldiesel-price-india-new-delhi.html
- **Indonesia:** http://www.bphmigas.go.id/p/bphmigaspages/bbm/daftar_harga_bbm.html
- **Japan:** http://oil-info.ieej.or.jp/price/price_ippan_kyuyujo_syuji.html
- **Malaysia:** http://www.petrolmalaysia.com/
- **New Zealand:** http://www.aa.co.nz/motoring/owning/running-costs/petrolwatch/Pages/default.aspx
- **Philippines:** http://www.doe.gov.ph/OPM/Archives.htm
- **Singapore:** http://www.petrolwatch.com.sg/
- **South Korea:** http://www.opinet.co.kr
- **Taiwan:** http://www.cpc.com.tw/big5_BD/tmtd/ListPrice/ShowListPrice_E.asp?pno=107&showtype=1
- **Thailand:** http://www.pttplc.com/en/nc_oi.aspx
- **Vietnam:** http://www.petrolimex.com.vn/Desktop.aspx/Home-En

(vi) Correlation between Petrol prices & Car mileage claim rate - Correlation

- **Correlation:** A correlation value close to 1 implies a strong positive relationship between the 2 data sets. A value close to -1 implies a strong negative relationship. A value of 0 implies no relationship. The correlation between Petrol prices & Car mileage claim rate is 0.34, signifying that there is a positive relationship between Petrol prices & Car mileage claim rate.
- R^2: R^2 values close to 1 implies a close fit between the trendline and data points. The R^2 value for Petrol prices is 0.8038, whereas, the R^2 value for Car mileage claim is 0.1428.

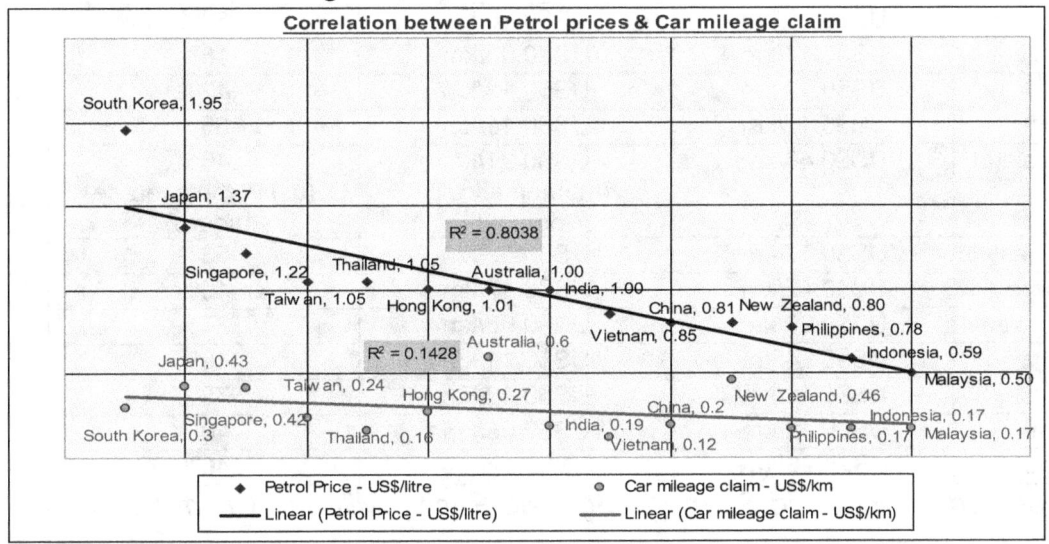

Source: Cedric Ng Mong Shen (2009) Asia-Pacific Mileage Claim Survey Report, 2019 September 8.

(vii) Relationship between Car & Motorcycle mileage claim rate

On average, motorcycle mileage claim quantum is 46% of car mileage claim quantum. Using this relationship, the New Zealand motorcycle mileage claim is derived from the car mileage claim.

Country	Median mileage claim		Relationship between Car & Motorcycle mileage claim quantum
	Car (US$/ km)	Motorcycle (US$/ km)	
Australia	US$0.60/km	US$0.25/km	42%
China	US$0.20/km	US$0.10/km	50%
Hong Kong	US$0.27/km	US$0.11/km	41%
India	US$0.19/km	US$0.10/km	53%
Indonesia	US$0.17/km	US$0.03/km	18%
Japan	US$0.43/km	US$0.18/km	42%
Malaysia	US$0.17/km	US$0.11/km	65%
New Zealand	US$0.46/km	US$0.21/km (mathematically derived)	46% (using the average figure)
Philippines	US$0.17/km	US$0.09/km	53%
Singapore	US$0.42/km	US$0.17/km	40%
South Korea	US$0.30/km	US$0.08/km	27%
Taiwan	US$0.24/km	US$0.11/km	46%
Thailand	US$0.16/km	US$0.12/km	75%
Vietnam	US$0.12/km	US$0.05/km	46%
Average	**US$0.26/km**	**US$0.12/km**	**46%**

Source: Cedric Ng Mong Shen (2009) Asia-Pacific Mileage Claim Survey Report, 2019 September 8.

(viii) Winter Clothing benefits – by Country

Companies providing winter clothing benefit.

Country	Companies not providing winter clothing benefit	Companies providing winter clothing benefit	Total sample
Singapore	56% (19 companies)	44% (15 companies)	34 companies
Malaysia	62% (13 companies)	38% (8 companies)	21 companies
Philippines	67% (9 companies)	33% (3 companies)	12 companies
Thailand	77% (10 companies)	23% (3 companies)	13 companies
Indonesia	79% (11 companies)	21% (3 companies)	14 companies
Vietnam	87% (8 companies)	13% (1 company)	9 companies
Bangladesh	87% (7 companies)	13% (1 company)	8 companies
China	87% (13 companies)	13% (2 companies)	15 companies
Korea	90% (9 companies)	10% (1 company)	10 companies
India	90% (9 companies)	10% (1 company)	10 companies
Australia	91% (10 companies)	9% (1 company)	11 companies
Japan	91% (10 companies)	9% (1 company)	11 companies
Taiwan	91% (10 companies)	9% (1 company)	11 companies
Hong Kong	92% (11 companies)	8% (1 company)	12 companies

Source: Cedric Ng Mong Shen (2009) Asia-Pacific Winter Clothing Benefit Survey Report, 2019 September 8.

Winter clothing benefit quantum.

Country	Sample size	Winter clothing benefit quantum.				
		Minimum	Lower quartile	Median	Upper quartile	Maximum
Singapore	15 companies	US$100	US$183	US$265	US$330	US$465
Philippines	3 companies	US$100	US$113	US$125	US$173	US$220
Malaysia	8 companies	US$96	US$100	US$110	US$202	US$465
Thailand	3 companies	US$100	US$100	US$100	US$106	US$112
Indonesia	3 companies	US$100	US$100	US$100	US$183	US$265
Vietnam	1 company	-	-	US$100	-	-
Bangladesh	1 company	-	-	US$100	-	-
Korea	1 company	-	-	US$100	-	-
Australia	1 company	-	-	US$100	-	-
India	1 company	-	-	US$100	-	-
Japan	1 company	-	-	US$100	-	-
Taiwan	1 company	-	-	US$100	-	-
Hong Kong	1 company	-	-	US$100	-	-
China	2 companies	US$73	US$80	US$87	US$93	US$100

Source: Cedric Ng Mong Shen (2009) Asia-Pacific Winter Clothing Benefit Survey Report, 2019 September 8.

(viii) Winter period & temperature – by country

As employees based in cities that have winter are usually not eligible for winter clothing benefit, this section shows the winter period and temperature range of Asia-pacific countries based on primary research.

Country	City	Winter period	Temperature range in a year
Australia	Sydney	**Winter**: Jun to Aug	8 to 26 °C
	Melbourne	**Winter**: Jun to Aug	6 to 26 °C
Bangladesh	Dhaka	**Winter**: Oct to Mar	11 to 32 °C
China	Beijing	**Winter**: Nov to Mar	- 9 to 31 °C
	Shanghai	**Winter**: Dec to Feb	1 to 31 °C
	GuangZhou	**Winter**: Dec to Feb	10 to 32 °C
	Tianjin	**Winter**: Nov to Mar	- 9 to 31 °C
	Zhuhai	**Winter**: Dec to Feb	10 to 32 °C
Hong Kong	Hong Kong	**Winter**: Jan to Mar	14 to 31 °C
India	Bangalore	**Winter**: Oct to Feb	16 to 33 °C
	New Delhi	**Winter**: Nov to Mar	7 to 39 °C
Japan	Tokyo	**Winter**: Dec to Feb	6 to 25 °C
Korea	Seoul	**Winter**: Nov to Mar	- 4 to 30 °C
Taiwan	Taipei	**Winter**: Nov to Feb	12 to 33 °C
Indonesia	Jakarta	**No Winter**	23 to 31 °C
Malaysia	Kuala Lumpur	**No Winter**	23 to 32 °C
Philippines	Makati City	**No Winter**	23 to 32 °C
Singapore	Singapore	**No Winter**	23 to 32 °C
Thailand	Bangkok	**No Winter**	23 to 35 °C
Vietnam	Hanoi	**No Winter**	21 to 34 °C

Website source:

- *Australia:*
  http://www.ausemade.com.au/national/resource/climate/cities.htm
- *Bangladesh:*
  http://www.weatheronline.co.uk/reports/climate/Bangladesh.htm
  http://www.climate-zone.com/climate/bangladesh/celsius/rangpur.htm
- *China (Beijing):*
  http://www.travelchinaguide.com/cityguides/beijing/when-to-go.htm
  http://www.climate-zone.com/climate/china/celsius/beijing.htm
- *China (Shanghai):*

http://www.asiarooms.com/travel-guide/china/shanghai/shanghai-overview/shanghai-weather.html
http://www.climate-zone.com/climate/china/celsius/shanghai.htm
- China (GuangZhou):
http://www.asiarooms.com/travel-guide/china/guangzhou/guangzhou-overview/guangzhou-weather.html
http://www.climate-zone.com/climate/china/celsius/guangzhou.htm
- China (Tianjin):
http://www.travelchinaguide.com/cityguides/beijing/when-to-go.htm
http://www.climate-zone.com/climate/china/celsius/beijing.htm
- China (Zhuhai):
http://www.asiarooms.com/travel-guide/china/guangzhou/guangzhou-overview/guangzhou-weather.html
http://www.climate-zone.com/climate/china/celsius/guangzhou.htm
- Hong Kong:
http://www.discoverhongkong.com/seasia/trip-planner/hongkong-weather.html
http://www.climate-zone.com/climate/china/celsius/hong-kong-intl-arpt.htm
- India (Bangalore):
http://www.asiarooms.com/travel-guide/india/bangalore/bangalore-overview/bangalores-weather.html
http://www.climate-zone.com/climate/india/celsius/bangalore.htm
- India (New Delhi):
http://www.asiarooms.com/travel-guide/india/delhi/delhi-overview/weather-of-delhi.html
http://www.climate-zone.com/climate/india/celsius/delhi.htm
- Japan:
http://www.jnto.go.jp/eng/arrange/essential/climate.html
- Korea:
http://english.visitkorea.or.kr/enu/AK/AK_EN_1_1_2.jsp
http://www.climate-zone.com/climate/south-korea/celsius/seoul-city.htm
- Taiwan:
http://eng.taiwan.net.tw/m1.aspx?sNo=0002005
http://www.climate-zone.com/climate/taiwan/celsius/taipei-city.htm

- *Indonesia:*
  http://www.climate-zone.com/climate/indonesia/celsius/jakarta-observatory.htm
- *Malaysia:*
  http://www.climate-zone.com/climate/malaysia/celsius/malacca.htm
- *Philippines:*
  http://www.climate-zone.com/climate/philippines/celsius/manila.htm
- *Singapore:*
  http://www.climate-zone.com/climate/singapore/celsius/singapore.htm
- *Thailand:*
  http://www.climate-zone.com/climate/thailand/celsius/bangkok.htm
- *Vietnam:*
  http://www.climate-zone.com/climate/vietnam/celsius/ho-chi-minh.htm

12) How to review employee benefits – Method 1

12.1) Benefits Review Example 1: Brunei employee benefits proposal

Terms	Brunei Statutory requirement & market practice	Proposal
Annual leave	• **Legal minimum:** 7 days for 1st year, increasing by 1 day each year up to 14 days. • **Market practice:** 12 days to 20 days, depending on level, for first year.	18 days annual leave for Exempts (Align with APAC HQ)
Medical	Bruneians & PRs are provided free medical at all Brunei Government Hospital & Clinic.	Not necessary as medical is provided free in Brunei.
Insurance	Compulsory to purchase Local Workman Compensation Insurance in Brunei.	USD29 per employee (20% mark-up from APAC HQ Workman Compensation Insurance rate of USD24 per employee).
Social security	• **Tabung Amanah Pekerja (TAP) contribution:** Every month, employees who are residents and citizens of the country will have 5% of their salary deducted for their retirement savings in TAP, another 5% is topped up by their employers. It is the employer's responsibility to deduct and pay the contribution to TAP over the counter. • **Supplemental Contributory Pensions (SCP) contribution:** .5% contributed by the employee from his monthly salary and the employer is required to contribute with the same rate of 3.5% per month. Source: http://www.mof.gov.bn/index.php/divisions/scp	Follow Brunei law: (1) TAP contribution = 5% of basic contributed both by employer and employee individually (2) SCP contribution = 3.5% of basic contributed both by employer and employee individually

12.2 Benefits Review Example 2: Singapore employee benefits proposal

Staff benefits	Company's current practice	Statutory minimum	Market practice	Proposal	Cost impact of change
Annual leave	14 days annual leave per year	7 days annual leave per year	16 days annual leave per year	Propose to increase annual leave from 14 to 16 days per year, to be competitive with the market practice.	Cost impact is $20,000 per year ((16 – 14 additional annual leave days) x 100 staff X $100 average staff salary per day]
Birthday voucher	Nil	Not mandatory	50% of companies provide $50 cash vouchers on staff's birthday	Propose to give $50 cash vouchers on employee's birthday to boost staff engagement.	Cost impact is $500 per year ($50 cash voucher x 100 staff)
Health screening	Staff can claims up to $200 for health screening every year.	Not mandatory	$300 per year for health screening claims	$300 per year for health screening claims to improve staff health.	Cost impact is $10,000 per year (($300 – $200 additional health screening claims) x 100 staff]
Sick leave	30 days sick leave per year	14 days sick leave per year	14 days sick leave per year.	Propose to reduce the sick leave entitlement from 30 days to 14 days, to be in line with market, and reduce company cost.	Last year, only 10 staff out of 500 staff took more than 14 days MC. Company cost savings of reducing the sick leave from 30 days to 14 days is $16,000 per year [(30 – 14 days sick leave) x 10 staff X $100 average staff salary per day].

13) How to review employee benefits – Method 2 (MPEP model)

A comprehensive approach to analyze and recommend employee benefits changes is to use the "MPEP model". In the MPEP model, employee benefits are analyzed from the perspectives of Market Position, Employee Preference, and Benefits Cost in a one-page graphical format. An important part of the MPEP approach is that it involves employees in decision making process via the benefits survey. Very often communicating a benefits program to employees is limited to management informing employees of their entitlements. Using the MPEP model, HR managers can easily help unions and employees understand the purpose and rationale of the company benefits made available to them in a one-page graphical format. Arrows in the MPEP model diagram shows the employee benefit item that the company is proposing to increase or decrease. In the MPEP diagram, the arrow is pointing upwards for annual leave because this company plans to increase its employee's annual leave benefit from below-market to above-market. "Market Position" refers to how a company's benefits compare with market practice. The rows of green boxes shows the company benefits that are "above-market", The rows of yellow boxes shows the company benefits that are "at-market", The rows of red boxes shows the company benefits that are "below-market". "Benefits cost" shows the cost/value of the company's staff benefits. Employee Preference shows the company benefits that employees value most. "Employee Preference" is measured via benefits survey, whereby employees need to rank all the existing and proposed company benefits from most important to least important. Employee Preference rating of "1" means that employees value this company benefit most. In the diagram, Annual leave and Product discounts have an Employee Preference rating of "1" – this means that employees of this company value Annual leave and Product discounts benefits most.

Figure 2: MPEP model

Proposed changes to employee benefits (using MPEP Benefits analysis)

The arrows shows the Staff benefit items that the company is proposing to increase or decrease based on market practice, importance of the benefit item to XX company staff (based on views of XX company staff who participated in the benefits survey), & cost of that particular benefit to company.

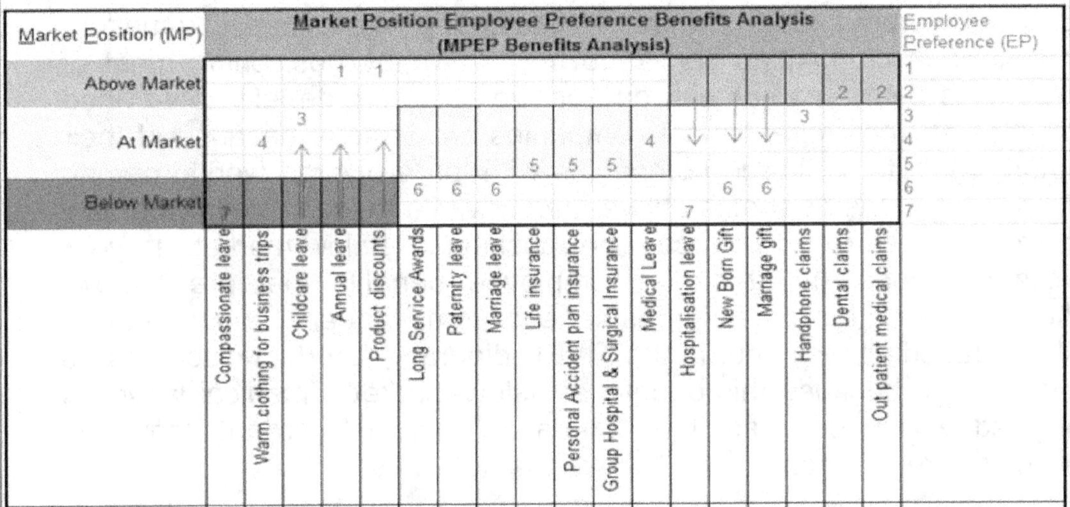

Market Position (MP)	Market Position Employee Preference Benefits Analysis (MPEP Benefits Analysis)															Employee Preference (EP)
Above Market			1	1									2	2		1 / 2
At Market	4	↑	3 ↑	↑				5	5	4	↓	↓	3			3 / 4 / 5
Below Market					6	6	6				7	6	6				6 / 7
Benefit	Compassionate leave	Warm clothing for business trips	Childcare leave	Annual leave	Product discounts	Long Service Awards	Paternity leave	Marriage leave	Life insurance	Personal Accident plan insurance	Group Hospital & Surgical Insurance	Medical Leave	Hospitalisation leave	New Born Gift	Marriage gift	Handphone claims	Dental claims	Out patient medical claims	

		Benefits cost (no change)	$1,200	$1,500	$16,000	$260,000	$50,000	$2,000	$2,000	$3,000	$10,000	$1,200	$20,000	$18,000	$9,000	$4,000	$3,000	$9,600	$12,000	$40,000	$462,500
Benefits Costing		Benefits cost (With changes)	$1,200	$1,500	$20,000	$300,000	$200,000	$2,000	$2,000	$3,000	$10,000	$1,200	$20,000	$18,000	$4,500	$400	$600	$9,600	$12,000	$40,000	$646,000
		% Difference	0%	0%	25%	15%	300%	0%	0%	0%	0%	0%	0%	0%	-50%	-90%	-80%	0%	0%	0%	40%

13.1) "Market Position" (MP)

"Market Position" refers to how a company's compensation & benefits compares with market practice. Establish your benefits positioning by considering your unique company's circumstances such as: company affordability, ideal employee demographics, competitor practices, and business strategy/stage. Some companies differentiate by positioning their compensation above-market while positioning their benefits below-market. Cost-conscious companies can keep cost down by positioning most of their benefits below-market with one or two signature-benefits positioned above-market (remember...most companies are famous because of their signature benefits...). Large companies with large diverse workforce can position most of their benefits above-market while those benefits with low employee preference rating can be positioned below-market. If your benefits philosophy is at-market, employee benefits that are "below-market" can be enhanced, whereas benefits items that are "above-market" can be reduced or removed. In the MPEP diagram, "product discounts" is highlighted red because this benefit is "below-market". "medical leave" is highlighted yellow because it is "at-market", while "marriage leave" is highlighted "green" because it is "above-market".

A Global Benefits Philosophy should provide guidance on decision making, protect the organization from bad practice, and be broad enough to apply across different business units and countries. It should balance between global standardization and local customization. A company's budget also plays a large part in determining which benefits it can offer globally.

Employee Benefits such as share plans, product discounts, fitness benefits, recognition schemes, can be implemented worldwide, but others, such as retrenchment benefits and annual leave, will differ between countries based on local labor laws. Examples of Global Benefits Philosophies that can be applied across different business units and countries are:

- **To provide every employee worldwide with at least three-times salary life cover**, because we believe that it is important, and because we care about the dependents of our employees.

- **To provide every employee worldwide with work-life benefits above market median**. E.g. Work from home options for office workers.

- **To help employees make friends at work worldwide**. E.g. through Free snacks at pantry, Buddy system, Team building events, staff birthday celebrations, Skype.

- **To make recognition part of our culture worldwide.** E.g. Provide Recognitions options (Thank you email templates), Share recognition ideas (E.g. Drive by to visit your colleagues to catch up with their lives, handwritten recognition notes, grab a team member for a quick walk and talk over coffee).

- **To position our Employee Wellness Benefits worldwide, above market median.** E.g. Hydraulic Tables for office employees, Dependent benefits, Free family counseling hotline, Health/Stress Talks, Under-Desk cycling exercise machine memento for employee of the month.

- **To provide signature mementos for every employee worldwide.** E.g. Miniature Volvo Truck mementos, or Volvo Cars shaped thumb drive mementos for all new employees.

13.2) "Employee Preference" (EP)

"Employee Preference" is measured via benefits survey, whereby employees need to rank the staff benefits from most important to least important. All the benefits must be ranked because feedback such as "All the benefits are equally important to me", is useless for decision making. Benefits that are rated highly by most employees can be enhanced, whereas benefits items that are rated lowly by most employees can be reduced or removed. If product discounts is rated "1" for "Employee Preference", it means that most employees voted product discounts as their most preferred benefit. Employee preference is affected by your company's current employee demographics. If your company has many older employees, benefits such as retirement plan is likely to be rated "1" for employee preference. However, if your company's HR strategy is to hire more younger employees, you can decide not to increase retirement plan benefits although it is highly rated by most of its current employees. Benefits should be designed to attract the segment that the company wants to hire & retain.

13.3) "Benefits Costing"

"Benefits Costing" refers to estimating the cost of the company's staff benefits. Benefits that are expensive are less likely to be adopted than benefits that are less costly.

13.4) "Arrows"

"Arrows" in the MPEP Benefits analysis diagram shows the employee benefit item that the company is proposing to increase or decrease. In the MPEP diagram, the arrow is pointing upwards for annual leave because this company plans to increase its employee's annual leave benefit.

14) Conclusion.

The "MPEP model" factors needs to be considered in totality. If annual leave is "red" for "market position" and "1" for "Employee Preference", companies might want to increase this benefit item because it means that its annual leave is below-market and their employees highly value this benefit. However, if the "Benefits Cost" of giving employees additional annual leave is too costly, companies might finally decide not to increase annual leave. Many companies do not realize the significance of an organization's benefits on Business strategy, Employer Branding, & HR strategy. Offering free or discounted company products to employees is one of the best "benefits-to-company" as it motivates employees, enhance employee's product knowledge, and generate business for employers themselves. Hotels that offer their employees free hotel stay, allow their staff to enjoy the hotel facilities that they work in, and help to enhance their product knowledge. It also generates business for the hotel as staff often wants their family and friends to experience their company's product/service. Employer branding requires taking bold steps to create signature-benefits and ensure the benefits program are tailored towards the firm's unique employee profile. An important part of the MPEP approach is that it involves employees in decision making process via the benefits survey. With the "MPEP model" approach, management can easily help employees understand the rationale of the company benefits in a one-page graphical format from the MPEP perspective of market-position, employee-preference, signature-benefits & benefits-cost. If you take these tips to heart and apply them within your organization, you increase the likelihood that you'll have happy, motivated employees who are proud to be in a company famous for its signature benefits!

Publications by the Author

https://www.amazon.com/s?k=ng+mong+shen
https://www.facebook.com/thehrdiary/

https://www.amazon.com/dp/B07TW7V7F5/

A lot of organizational data is often untapped unstructured data in the form of text & numbers. For those who don't want to spend months learning R programming & for those who can't afford to buy expensive SPSS statistical software. This is the only book that teaches you how to use Microsoft Excel for Predictive HR Analytics, Text Mining & Organizational Network Analysis (ONA) with step-by-step print-screen instructions:

1) Predictive HR Analytics: Use Excel's Statistical Analysis tools (Decision trees, Correlation, Multiple & Logistic Regression) to run Predictive HR Analytics. E.g. an employee is predicted to have a 60% probability of getting into accidents, if he is age 25, worked 1 year in the company & took 6 days sick leave. An employee is predicted to get rated "7" for Customer Service, if the training program that he attended has a training evaluation score of "8". An employee is predicted to resign if she is age 23, worked for 2 years, and takes 60 minutes to commute to work.

2) Organizational Network Analysis (ONA): Run ONA using Excel's network analysis tool. Learn how to convert an employee's organizational network into a score & then predict if they will be a high-potential (HiPo). E.g. an employee is predicted to be a HiPo with performance rating of "9", if his "Social Network Size" is "16", "Social Network Diversity Index" is "3" & "Competency Score" is "8".

3) Text Mining, Sentiment Analysis & Word Clouds: Mine text from social network posts, employee engagement surveys & Glassdoor comments, then run Sentiment Analysis using Excel & visualize the insights with "Word Clouds". Learn how to predict a company's average employee attrition rate based on its sentiment. E.g. a company's average employee attrition rate is predicted to be 8%, if unemployment rate is 3%, GDP growth is 2%, Glassdoor public sentiment rating is "5", and engagement score is "7".

https://www.amazon.com/Predictive-HR-Analytics-Mong-Shen/dp/1790406374/

You don't need to spend months learning the Python, R or SQL programming language, and you don't need to buy expensive statistical software like SPSS or SAS. This is the only book that teaches you Predictive Analytics using Microsoft Excel (which you already have & know how to use)! This book not only share with you the analytics findings of other companies, but also teaches you how to derive it by yourself! It covers the ARHAT Predictive HR Analytics framework, teaches you data-storytelling & data-visualization techniques, and teaches you how to use Microsoft Excel's statistical tools (Decision trees, Correlation, Multiple Regression, Logistic Regression, Chi-Square) with step-by-step print-screen instructions. It is also the only book that covers the full HR Analytics scope (Benefits, Compensation, Culture, Diversity & Inclusion, Engagement, Leadership, Learning & Development, Payroll, Personality Traits, Performance Management, Recruitment, Sales Incentives) with numerous real-world Predictive HR Analytics examples, & shows how Predictive HR Analytics answers questions such as:

(1) Predict who are the people at risk of leaving using Decision tree, Correlation, Excel Logistic Regression, etc. (e.g. employee aged 30, who stays more than xx km from the company, who is rated "average for performance", has a 90% probability of resigning in her 3rd year.).

(2) Identify where the best people come from and how successful a candidate will be if hired using simple correlation (E.g. Customer Service staff and Sales staff with x & y personality traits are likely to be good performers if hired).

(3) Predict impact of Employee Engagement on customer satisfaction, revenue and Shareholder Returns, etc. using Excel Multiple Regression. (e.g. 1% increase in employee engagement leads to $100k increase in company revenue, 2% increase in customer satisfaction, 1% increase in Shareholders return, 1 day reduction in average sick leave, etc.).

(4) Predict financial impact of training using Excel Multiple Regression (e.g. training satisfaction rating of xx leads to $y increase in company revenue).

(5) Predict Diversity & Inclusion's impact on revenue and EBIT (e.g. convert your company's ethnic diversity mix to an index number, then use Excel Multiple Regression to predict if your company's diversity Index is x --> your company's Sales will be $y and EBIT will be z%).

(6) Predict employee absenteeism and accident, using Chi-Square.

https://www.amazon.com/dp/B07PXRLL3Z/

You don't need to buy expensive statistical software like SPSS. This book teaches you R (R can be downloaded for free), People Analytics, Social Media Analytics, Text Mining and Sentiment Analysis. It is written for people with no knowledge of R, with step-by-step print-screen instructions. You don't need Statistical knowledge, as R executes the statistical number crunching (Correlation, Multiple & Logistic Regression, etc.) for you, by simply entering a few commands. This book covers the full People Analytics scope (Benefits, Compensation, Culture, Diversity & Inclusion, Engagement, Leadership, Learning & Development, Personality Traits, Performance Management, Recruitment, Sales Incentives) with numerous real-world examples, and shows how **R** can help you:

1) Run Social Media Analytics, Text mining & Sentiment Analysis with R.

2) Predict employees' flight-risk using R's Correlation & Logistic Regression function.

3) Identify the personality traits of top performing Customer Service staff and Sales staff using R's correlation function.

4) Predict impact of Employee Engagement on Customer Satisfaction, Revenue and Shareholder Returns, etc. using R's Correlation & Multiple Regression function.

5) Predict impact of Learning & Development on Sales, using R's Multiple Regression function.

6) Predict Diversity & Inclusion's impact on Revenue and EBIT using R's Multiple Regression function.

https://www.amazon.com/Designing-Global-Sales-Incentive-Plans-ebook/dp/B07FW14LFZ/

Your company has hundreds of patchwork sales incentive plans developed by various business units after decades of mergers & acquisitions. Sales incentive plans for B2C sales is not effective to drive performance for B2B sales, and frequently individual sales quotas are not set properly. As the Global Rewards Director, you are assigned by your CEO to reduce the number of sales incentive plans and align it to corporate strategy. Do you know what to do?

The key to designing an effective global sales-compensation framework is to identify performance measures and design principles that can apply globally and yet provide some flexibility for business unit or local customization. This book teaches you a nine step, 3D6P approach to design effective global sales incentive plans (Diagnose the root cause of poor sales, Determine change management strategy, Determine eligibility, Pay strategy, Performance measures, Plan mechanics, Payout scenario, Plan documentation & communication, Plan effectiveness). The concepts and examples in this book, works for all companies of all sizes, in all industries. The concept is comprehensive and yet flexible. Companies can choose to use all or parts of the steps to design their sales incentive plan.

https://www.amazon.com/Organization-Design-Performance-Step-Step-ebook/dp/B07GFSN93Y/

Organizations must be able to adapt their structures to capture new markets and expand existing ones. The design that works during start-up is different from what works during growth, maturity, and decline. However, when Companies are not structured properly, business opportunities fizzle due to lack of attention, and turf wars stifle teamwork because of unclear responsibilities. Often Performance issues are a Structural issue rather than a Person issue. A company can have great people, great leadership and still not perform well because of poor organizational design.

Organization design is more than moving the boxes. It is about how to configure your Department or Company structure to improve performance, and can be applied by Department managers at all levels. Organization Design work sometimes encompasses redesign of an entire company, but mostly the focus is at departmental level.

This book highlights the warning signs when organization design is needed, and provides a simple four-step framework to guide managers how to design effective Departments and Organizations:
• Step 1 – Define Criteria
• Step 2 – Diagnose Issues
• Step 3 – Design Structure
• Step 4 – Deliver Structure

https://www.amazon.com/Designing-Salary-Structures-Step-Step-ebook/dp/B07G264J11/

Your CEO returned from a management retreat with a new strategic business plan that will revitalize the company and lead it into lucrative new markets. As the Director of Compensation and Benefits, you are charged with translating the strategic business plan into a pay strategy that supports the company's vision and business strategy. Do you know what to do?

To design the Salary structures that drive business results and performance, you need to know which positions are "hot skills", which positions are difficult-to-hire, which positions have high attrition rate, and which functions are strategic functions. Each of these has implications for designing a salary structure that drives business results and performance. Salary structures provide guidelines for making pay related decisions within an organization, bridging the gap between where you are today and where you want to be tomorrow (target pay positioning).

This book shows you in six simplified steps, how to design strategic salary structures:
1) Establish your pay positioning.
2) Establish job worth hierarchy.
3) Develop job grades.
4) Develop pay range.
5) Calculate structural parameters (pay range, min, max).
6) "Slot" your employees and tweak your salary structure

https://www.amazon.com/dp/B0859CB567/

Best Buy can predict that a 0.1% increase in employee engagement results in $100,000 increase in income. Though Amazon didn't promise a heart-warming employee experience & didn't promise work-life balance, it is among the top organizations in employee satisfaction. This is the only book that incorporates Employee Experience & Engagement with Predictive Analytics, & offers a new way to cultivate engagement using **"4 Engagement Bags"**:

Bag 1) Inspire with Engagement Investment: Inspire with Predictive Analytics, and Inspire with Stories & Data Visualisation Techniques & predict the impact of Employee Engagement on Revenue using Excel Correlation & Regression

Bag 2) Inspire with Engagement Fertilizers: Making employees happy, doesn't mean they will work hard for the organization. Use the 5 "Engagement Fertilizers" to build great employee experience & engagement:
- **Fertilizer 1: Basic Needs** – Soil, Rain, Sun
- **Fertilizer 2: Social Needs** – Birds
- **Fertilizer 3: Growth Needs** – Nutrients
- **Fertilizer 4: Meaning** – Healthy Tree
- **Fertilizer 5: Expectations** – Fruits!

Bag 3) Sentiment Gathering: Pulse Surveys, Focus Groups, Glassdoor Reviews, IISS Engagement Diagnosis Questions.

Bag 4) Sentiment Diagnosis & Prescription: Engagement Metrics & Dashboards, Bar & Radar Charts, Correlation, Regression & IISS Engagement Prescriptions, Sentiment Analysis with "Azure Machine Learning" & Word Clouds.

Index

A

Absenteeism, 11
Annual leave, 55

B

Bag 1, 98
Bag 2, 98
Basic Needs, 98
Brunei employee benefits, 82
Business impact, 11
Business Stage, 18
Business Strategy, 18

C

Categories of Benefits, 42
Clinical Care Coverage, 60
Company Branding, 17
Costs, 22, 23

D

Death benefits, 49
Defined benefit (DB) plans, 50
Defined contribution (DC) plans, 51
Demographic, 22, 23
Dental plans, 48
Disability benefits, 49

E

Employee's potential, 17
Expectations, 98

F

Factors influencing Benefits Globally, 22

Flexi-benefits, 21

G

Glassdoor, 19
Global Benefits Strategies, 17
Google, 13
Growth Needs, 98

H

Healthcare benefits, 42, 43
Hearing plans, 48
Hewlett-Packard, 13
Hybrid plans, 51
Hygiene factors, 8

I

Income protection, 42
Income Protection Plans, 43
Industry practice, 22, 23
Inspire with Engagement Fertilizers, 98
Inspire with Engagement Investment, 98

J

Job Grade, 18
Job Satisfaction, 12

L

Labor Laws, 22, 23
Life and Disability Insurance, 60

M

Maternity leave, 57
Meal benefits, 34, 35
Meaning, 98

Medical plans, 48
Motivation factors, 8
MPEP, 84

P

Pay for time not worked, 42
Perceived value, 22, 23
Performance, 11

R

Reading employees benefits survey reports, 58, 61
Retention, 13
Retirement and investment plans, 42
Retirement and Investment Plans, 50

S

Sentiment Diagnosis & Prescription, 98

Sentiment Gathering, 98
Share ownership, 12
Sick leave, 56
Signature benefits, 19
Singapore employee benefits, 83
Social Needs, 98

T

Tax laws, 22, 25
Trade Blocs, 22, 24
Transport benefits, 25

V

Vision plans, 48

W

Welfare benefits, 42, 49

www.ingramcontent.com/pod-product-compliance
Lightning Source LLC
Chambersburg PA
CBHW060427220526
45465CB00008B/3041